Putting It Together

Putting It Together
Middle School Math in Transition

Gary Tsuruda

Jordan Middle School
Palo Alto, CA

HEINEMANN
Portsmouth, NH

Heinemann
A division of Reed Elsevier Inc.
361 Hanover Street   Portsmouth, NH 03801-3912
Offices and agents throughout the world

Acquisitions Editor: Toby Gordon
Production Editor: Renée M. Pinard
Cover Designer: Jenny Jensen Greenleaf

Library of Congress Cataloging-in-Publication Data

Tsuruda, Gary.
    Putting it together : middle school math in transition / Gary Tsuruda.
        p.   cm.
    Includes bibliographical references (p.   –   ).
    ISBN 0-435-08355-4
    1. Mathematics—Study and teaching (Secondary).   I. Title.
QA11.T85   1994
510.71'2—dc20   93-46755
                                                                    CIP

Printed in the United States of America on acid-tree paper
99 98 97 96 95 94   EB   1 2 3 4 5 6

To Mom and Dad,
with love and respect

Contents

Preface   ix

Acknowledgments   xiii

Chapter One   *The Seeds of Change*   1

Chapter Two   *Paradigm Shift*   5

Chapter Three   *Solving Problems*   13

Chapter Four   *Student Writing*   59

Chapter Five   *Assessment Alternatives*   79

Chapter Six   *Grouping Practices*   93

Chapter Seven   *Putting It Together*   105

References   111

Preface

The current revolution in mathematics education is the single most significant change in mathematics pedagogy since the New Math upheaval of the 1960s. Like its predecessor, the current reform movement is based on a firm belief that massive change is not only desirable but urgently necessary. Reformers claim that current educational practices do not prepare students to *do* mathematics.

There is a major difference, however, between the failed curriculum reform movement of the 1960s and its counterpart in the 1990s: where the New Math revolution was led by *mathematicians,* we are now basing our decisions on the research of math *educators.* The heart of the new reform movement is constructivism, a new way of looking at how students learn. The New Math philosophy that students should *understand* mathematical concepts rather than memorize procedures was both enlightened and revolutionary. Unfortunately, this ideal was translated into practice by simply asking "Why?" within a fairly traditional math program. We now know a great deal more about how students learn and how the brain works. Recent research has shown that learning is the construction of knowledge and that it has a very individual nature—that it depends on the understanding and beliefs each person brings to the learning situation.

Various pieces of the reform movement have evolved over the past several years, beginning with the publication of *A Nation at Risk* in 1983 and fueled by an increasing awareness of the vastly more complex needs of the work force in the twenty-first century. The establishment of the Mathematical Sciences Education Board (MSEB) in 1985 and the National Council of Teachers of Mathematics (NCTM) Commission on Standards for School Mathematics in 1986 led to the publication of two significant documents: *Everybody Counts,* published in 1989 by the MSEB, eloquently outlines the need for reform, and the NCTM's *Curriculum and Evaluation Standards for School Mathematics* gives substance to this outline by establishing national standards. A number of other publications have supported the need for reform, including the MSEB's *Reshaping School Mathematics,* published in 1990.

The themes of these documents are consistent not simply among themselves but with current learning theorists and researchers (see, for example, Lauren Resnick's *Education and Learning to Think*). They highlight the need to change how we provide instruction for students based on a completely different view of how students learn. This new learning philosophy drives the reform movement in mathematics, and it is only by personally accepting this new paradigm that teachers will begin to transform their teaching and to make mathematics interesting and meaningful for their students.

I recently took part in a process that had a significant impact on my teaching. From 1988 through 1991, I was a member of the committee that helped develop the 1992 *Mathematics Framework for California Public Schools.* The *Framework* is intended to guide and support schools in California as they begin to change their mathematics programs. It describes the dimensions of mathematical power and identifies characteristics of mathematical programs that empower students mathematically. In addition to suggesting unifying ideas for mathematical content, the *Framework* provides the philosophical spirit for reform.

The committee met for two days each month to discuss which issues the new framework should address. Although we represented a variety of roles in the educational community—classroom teachers, university professors, math project leaders, administrators—we shared a commitment to improving mathematics instruction for all students. Our debates were lively, and we often agreed to disagree on certain issues, but over time a common vision of math education emerged.

I felt that my own role in the framework process was to represent middle school classroom teachers. I had used many of the ideas we were discussing—and had used them successfully—in my classroom. Those real classroom experiences made it easy for me to contribute to most of the discussions. However, some of the ideas were difficult to understand, let alone agree with. My experience didn't include a constructivist view of learning or heterogeneously grouped classes or portfolio assessment. In the process of struggling with these ideas and trying to make sense of them in the real world of my classroom, I have undergone a transformation that is part of and yet transcends the modifications I have been making in my teaching over the past several years. It wasn't until I understood constructivism and tried heterogeneous grouping that it all came together for me.

Acknowledgments

So many people have contributed to my growth and personal transition as a math teacher that it would be impossible to thank them all here. My teaching colleagues at Bowditch Middle School in Foster City, Abbott Middle School in San Mateo, and JLS and Jordan Middle Schools in Palo Alto have provided great ideas and encouragement throughout my teaching career. I appreciate their generosity and their support.

I would like to acknowledge one group of educators in particular for the immense impact they have had on my thinking. The fourteen members of the California State Framework Committee, through their dedication to math education and their determination to stand up for what they believe is right, have been a catalyst for change in my teaching. I am especially grateful to Ruth Cossey for her friendship and continued support of me as a teacher. She has always been two steps ahead of me and has challenged me to keep up.

I would also like to thank Bill Kramer for his leadership, support, and mentoring. We didn't always agree, but through our discussions, we developed a lifelong respect and friendship.

Teachers are defined to some extent by their students, and I've been fortunate enough to have known and taught thousands of wonderful students. I can only hope that they have learned as much from me as I have from them. Their energy, creativity, and original thinking have enlightened me over and over through the years.

And finally I would like to thank my wife, Nellie, and my daughters, Cheryl and Cathy, for being patient with me and understanding that the many hours I spend on my teaching does not in any way diminish my love for them.

The Seeds of Change 1

Seven years ago, I thought I knew how to teach mathematics. I had been teaching middle school math for seventeen years and had kept myself abreast of current developments in the field through professional conferences and readings. I prided myself on my work ethic and my ability to relate to middle school students. In fact, I gave workshops for other teachers on such topics as motivating students and organizing instruction. Colleagues often joked about my very detailed, left-brain-dominant lesson plans, which itemized the sequence of learning thoroughly and precisely.

I believed that mathematics, unlike most other subjects, is sequential and linear and can therefore best be taught through a clearly defined, well-organized series of steps presented to students whom we have motivated to succeed. In my classroom, this motivation took several forms, from congenial interaction with my students to math games, competitions, and group activities. We used manipulatives and calculators, and we had fun. The manipulatives were used to help teach skills, and the calculators were a motivational device to inspire students to learn to do pencil-and-paper computation. I introduced calculator "licenses," which I issued to individual students after they had mastered certain skills. Students with calculator licenses were even allowed to use their calculators on tests, a major innovation at the time.

I felt good about my teaching, and I believed my students were getting an excellent education. They were motivated and happy, and they were learning mathematics. But when I began to look more deeply into what my students were actually learning, I was troubled by what I saw.

My successful students were learning a mathematics that served them well in high school. Students who did well in the skill-based curriculum I presented did well in the rigid skill-based high school curriculum. The students were happy, I was happy, and the high school was happy. But what about those students who didn't succeed with me? They, of course, didn't succeed in high school either, and although I tended to rationalize their lack of success by telling myself they just "didn't have it," I felt bad and tried hard to create an environment in

1

which they could succeed. In retrospect, many of these students *would* have succeeded in the program I now teach. Because I was (and to a large extent still am) a left-brain-dominant, sequential thinker, I created a math program that was also left-brain-dominant and sequential. It seems clear to me now that my viewing mathematics in this way was a major factor in my attraction to the subject and to teaching.

Furthermore, the math I taught had little meaning for my students—even the good ones—outside the academic environment. I had always been troubled by discouraging reports about mathematics education (the National Assessment of Educational Progress [NAEP], for example), but I tended to externalize the poor results, thinking that things would have been different if *my* students had been assessed. Nevertheless, I think I knew deep down inside that if the students in my classes were tested a few months after they had "mastered" a certain skill, they would fare no better than those in the national sample. I knew, for example, that the work we had done with word problems in a traditional format had taught them more about recognizing problem structures than about solving problems. They learned to extract numbers from word problems, and they learned which operations applied to the patterns the numbers indicated.

Most of my students would have done no better than the nationwide sample of students asked this question: *There are 125 sheep and 5 dogs in a flock. How old is the shepherd?* Three out of four students across the nation responded with a numerical answer, the most common being that the shepherd's age is twenty-five. When I relate this question to math teachers and ask them to predict the results of the national sample, they are pretty accurate in their estimates. If anything, they are even more pessimistic about the abilities of our country's students. We are all aware of the problems facing math educators; we know that what we are doing isn't working, but we're not sure what to do to change it. Surely *not everything* is wrong with the current system, but clearly *something* is wrong. The current model of learning that views the teacher as dispenser, the student as passive receptacle, learning as accumulation, and knowledge as facts (cynically referred to as the tell-show-practice-test-and-forget model of learning) just doesn't produce mathematically powerful students. As much as I hate to admit it, I used this model for many years with hundreds of students, honestly believing that what I was doing was correct.

I wanted to motivate my students to continue to love and learn mathematics throughout their lives, but the motivation I worked so hard to instill was in many cases short-lived. My students were indeed motivated to do well and showed a genuine interest in mathematics, but that motivation and interest faded the next year and all but disappeared as they made their way through the high school curriculum. I took some pride in the fact that many students came back to me complaining about their successive teachers, saying how much fun they had had in my class. But I came to realize that, ego boost aside, such comments were a testimony to my failure as a teacher, not my success.

Those organized, sequential lessons I presented worked well in the skill-based curriculum of the 1970s, but as I tried to incorporate more problem solving and broader concepts into my teaching plans, I found the style just didn't fit. Unfortunately, this was not a realization I came to overnight. Like most paradigms, my view of how students learn was deeply ingrained in my teaching style, a style I had every reason to believe was successful. So I taught geometry and measurement and probability and even problem solving in an organized, sequential way. I told my students how to perform various skills associated with these strands; we practiced those skills; they "learned" them. When I look back on the kinds of things I used to do, especially with problem solving, I laugh. I know now that students do not learn to solve problems by memorizing a process.

It may have been my frustration with teaching problem solving that began to alter my thinking about teaching mathematics. When I finally began to see problem solving as a thinking process rather than a skill to be learned, I was forced to reexamine the other areas of mathematics as well. At first, I tried to rationalize the dissonance created by this realization. I talked myself into believing that mathematics is made up of a number of strands that consist of skills to be mastered. Once mastered, these skills assist us with the real business of mathematics, which is solving problems. This model seemed to work for me. However, much like the calculator licenses I used to issue, there was a built-in inconsistency with this model. When I issued calculator licenses, I was telling students that they had to master pencil-and-paper computation but once they proved they could do it, they wouldn't have to do it anymore; they could use the calculator. Similarly, I was telling students that problem solving was important, but I only gave them problems to solve after they had mastered certain skills in various areas of mathematics.

Over the past few years, my thinking about how students learn has changed significantly. I no longer believe that mathematics is a linear set of skills to be learned in order to solve problems. I no longer believe that students learn best when we present them with organized, sequential lessons wherein each skill has been task-analyzed. I no longer believe that it is enough to motivate students solely by what *I* do in my classroom. And I no longer believe that students need to learn skills as a prerequisite to solving problems. I have learned these lessons the hard way, through experiences with middle school students in the classroom.

Paradigm Shift 2

By educational standards, my shift from traditional teaching to my current approach appeared to have happened immediately. It seemed as if my entire view of teaching and learning underwent a major transformation in a period of several months, as if I had undergone some form of spiritual enlightenment. Indeed, the differences between the two philosophies are so dramatic that a change from one to the other is very much like "seeing the light." But change is a very slow process, especially in education; the transition was rapid only in relative terms.

Nor did I have a concurrent vision showing me what direction to take. Although many of the ideas I had been using for years fit nicely into the constructivist philosophy, it is only in the last few years that I have tried to align everything I do with this approach.

The major change in my view of teaching came as a result of discussions with other educators. These discussions helped me clarify my views and conceptualize the change in approach. It seems to me that the ability to accept change depends on a person's prior experience and how he or she views the need for change. This was certainly true for me. I had reached a stage in my teaching where I was eager— and able—to understand the ideas of other educators and begin to incorporate them into my thinking.

The traditional approach to education views the teacher as the dispenser of knowledge in the form of facts. Our classrooms are arranged to fit this model, with the teacher at the front of the room and the students in rows of desks trying to absorb the facts being dispensed. Each student performs the same set of rote procedures in order to arrive at the same conclusion.

However, we now view learning in much broader terms than this approach implies. The key to reform in mathematics education is a relatively new view of learning called constructivism, which maintains that students learn by constructing their own knowledge. This approach is based on the notion that each learner brings to the learning situation different sets of belief and understanding based on prior experience. By engaging in an activity in which he or she must construct learning by modifying previous ideas and beliefs, each learner comes away with a unique understanding of the concepts.

This is not to say that mutual agreement is not important. Certain facts, processes, and concepts are universal, and we would like all students to share a common understanding of them. However, different students may arrive at this understanding in different ways, depending on what they bring to the learning situation.

For example, consider the typical textbook approach to teaching students to find the area of a trapezoid. A situation is presented, the formula is quickly developed (or worse, simply given to the students), and sample problems show how to apply the formula to different trapezoids. Students are then given a series of exercises in which they are asked to find the area of various trapezoids, some of which provide only measurements and no drawing of the figure.

Contrast this with a more constructivist approach to the same concept (see Figure 2–1). Small groups of students are asked to discuss the meaning of *area* and *trapezoid* and to review what they know about how to find the area of other polygons. Then, still as a group, they are asked to find an easy way to determine the area of any trapezoid. They may be given hints to get them started if they have difficulty, and they are allowed to use graph paper, dot paper, calculators, and any other tools available in the classroom.

When I did this activity in my classroom, almost every group was able to come up with a formula for the area of a trapezoid in one class period. Not all the formulas looked like the typical textbook formula, but they were all correct, and more important, each formula made sense according to the way the students in that group had constructed the knowledge from the data they themselves had generated. And since the students had been asked to make sure their formula worked for all trapezoids, no page of exercises was necessary to ensure that they knew how to apply their formula.

This trapezoid "lesson" presented in the constructivist spirit took a little more than one class period because I also asked the students to write about how they got their formula and why the formula works, and I concluded the activity with class sharing and discussion. The traditional trapezoid lesson would have taken about the same amount of class time but would have cheated the students out of the opportunity to construct their own understanding of an important process. In addition, it would have been much less engaging for students and would have done nothing to foster the important skills of working coopera-

TRAPEZOID AREA

GOAL: Find an easy way to determine the area of any trapezoid.

Be sure that you understand the answers to each of these questions :
   1) What does "area" mean?
   2) What is a trapezoid?
   3) How do you find the area of other polygons? Show as many different ways as you can.

NOW SEE IF YOUR GROUP CAN FIND AN EASY WAY TO DETERMINE THE AREA OF ANY TRAPEZOID.

HINTS:
   1) Draw several trapezoids on dot paper and find their areas. Look for patterns.

   2) Consider how you find the area of other polygons. Are any of the key ideas similar?

   3) You might try cutting out trapezoids and piecing them together.

   4) If you find a way to determine the area, make sure that it is as easy as you can make it and that it works for <u>any</u> trapezoid.

WRITE-UP:
   1) *Explain your answers to the first three questions in detail. Tell how your group reached agreement on the answers.*

   2) *Tell what you did to get your formula for the area of any trapezoid. Did you use any of the hints? How did they help you?*

   3) *Show your formula and give an illustration of how it works.*

FIGURE 2–1

tively with other students and communicating mathematical understanding.

In a similar way, students can develop the formula for the area of a circle through a variety of experiments involving covering circles, weighing circle models, and cutting circles into pie-shaped pieces and rearranging them. As the class discusses their ideas and shares their formulas, each student will construct a personal knowledge of what it means to find the area of a circle. Giving students the formula is more expedient but ignores the lesson's essential purpose, the development of real understanding.

Researchers investigating how the brain grows and develops are finding data that supports the ideas behind constructivism. Many feel that the brain *needs* to construct patterns and make connections among disparate data in order for learning to occur. When we provide detailed, sequential procedures for students to follow, their brains are robbed of this opportunity. It's no wonder then that our wonderfully planned and detailed lesson plans often end in disappointment for both teacher and student.

In my view, understanding and accepting constructivist theory is much more important than using the practices we have come to associate with exemplary teaching. Heterogeneous classes, cooperative groups, journal writing, problem solving, calculator use, alternative assessment, and portfolios are all important and exciting components of the change in the way we approach mathematics instruction, but they represent the *form* rather than the *spirit* of the change.

In fact, some of the practices mentioned above make no sense in the context of a traditional approach. Portfolios, for example, are collections of student work over time. Students in a traditional math class would have little to include in their portfolio that might distinguish it from other students' portfolios. Likewise, problem solving taught as a set of procedures is of little value to students. These procedures help students solve a limited number of problems but deny them the opportunity to mull over, analyze, and synthesize the problems in order to create new strategies and processes for solving them.

This difference between the form and spirit of change is an inherent danger in any new approach to learning and teaching. It is quite possible for teachers to adopt new practices without changing their beliefs about learning. They may feel some pressure to be "politically correct"; or they may be forced by their administrators to incorporate these changes into their teaching. Unfortunately, going through the motions of reform without changing the beliefs upon which the practices are based may be worse than no change at all. The teacher is bound to be uncomfortable about doing something in which he or she doesn't believe, and the chances that a practice will succeed without the total support and enthusiasm of the teacher are limited; the door is left open for the teacher to announce, "I tried that and it didn't work." I support my fellow teachers' desire to make changes in their teaching by first emphasizing the need for change and the value of constructivism.

Certain teaching practices, most notably writing, can help teachers see the value of this new approach.

I used to feel that writing was for English teachers; my job was to teach mathematics and theirs was to teach writing. It never crossed my mind that writing could actually help me teach mathematics until some of my colleagues in other departments shared the experiences they had had when they asked their students to write about their learning.

I began by having students write summaries of units we had just completed. I was amazed at how much I learned about their understanding of concepts from this simple, relatively short writing assignment. I expanded this idea by having students write two-paragraph weekly or biweekly papers entitled "What I Understand and What I Don't Understand." Again, I was impressed by the amount of specific information I was able to gain from these essays. A unit test or weekly quizzes would have given me only a small fraction of that information.

These first essays made me see that I needed a new approach to instruction. I had always prided myself on sequential, task-analyzed lessons. If a student didn't understand a concept or a procedure, I'd explain it again in a different way, also well-planned and orderly. Unfortunately, not all students were successful. I rationalized that they were simply not motivated to learn. I reasoned that since my presentation was clear and sequential, I couldn't possibly blame myself for their failures. But when I read the unit summaries and the "What I Understand/Don't Understand" essays, I found that even the hardest-working, most-motivated students had misconceptions about and only partially understood the concepts I was teaching. I was forced to challenge my previous beliefs. A tidy, well-sequenced presentation wasn't good enough. I had to come up with alternatives to the traditional model.

I have increased the amount of writing I expect of students each year. Having students write about their learning has helped me develop a better understanding of *how* they learn and has strengthened my belief in constructivism. We often feel that we have a fairly accurate picture of what our students know, especially after we have corrected a test. In fact what a test usually gives us is a fairly incomplete picture of what our students *don't* know and almost no information about what they *do* know. Writing tells us so much more.

Students' writing is a window into their thinking. It allows us to see a truer picture of what students know and believe about particular concepts. For example, one year I assigned my sixth graders an essay in which they were to discuss which was bigger, 3/4 or 5/6. I could have simply included this on a test in the traditional form, asking them to fill in the blank with $>$, $<$, or $=$: 3/4 _____ 5/6. If I had done that, what would I have learned about those students who answered the question incorrectly? They indeed might not have understood which fraction is larger. On the other hand, they might have clearly understood the relative size of the two fractions but not the correct use of the symbols $>$ and $<$; or they might have made a computational error in analyzing the fractions. In addition, I might not have been correct in assuming that those students who filled in the blank with the correct symbol understood which fraction is larger. Some of them might simply have guessed correctly.

The essays students wrote (see the example in Figure 2–2) gave me clear insights into their understanding of fraction concepts, their ability to picture fractions, and their understanding of the relative size of fractions. Based on what we had done in class and the tests I had given them, I thought they all had very clear understandings of these concepts. I was surprised to find that some of the students had very little understanding of the basic concept of a fraction, that some of them were confused about common denominators, and that others drew pictures of fractions with unequal sizes or shapes.

This type of experience helped me clarify my beliefs about how students learn and laid the foundation for the changes in my thinking that were to take place over the next few years. My developing view of how children learn allowed me to make sense of the changes called for in the NCTM *Standards* and the California *Framework*. I was able to see the difference between the form and the spirit of the reform because of my understanding of this new view of learning.

1.
2.
$\frac{3}{4}$
$\frac{5}{6}$

As you can clearly see from the drawing above 5/6 is definitely bigger than 3/4. It is bigger here and it will always be bigger.

One way of proving this is that the benchmark for 5/6 is one, but the benchmark for 3/4 can either be ½ or one. Five-sixths is close to being a whole thing but three-fourths could be one-half or a whole.

Let's put this another way. Say you have a submarine sandwich. If you ate three-fourths you would be quite full. If you ate five-sixths of it you would probably get sick of the sandwich and throw it away. Submarine sandwiches are great but sometimes bigger is not better.

To think mathematically, you can subtract three-fourths from five-sixths, but subtracting five-sixths from three-fourths would surely give you a negative number. Trust me 5/6 is bigger!

FIGURE 2–2

Solving Problems 3

An easy and unobtrusive change any math teacher can make is to incorporate problem solving into the curriculum. Even those who have not yet begun to make problem solving a part of their teaching will find it fairly easy to do. I'd like to share a problem-solving format I've been using in my classes for over six years. I have been very pleased with the results. In fact, this approach to problem solving, along with writing, has been one of the most exciting and rewarding things I have done in all my years of teaching.

Behavioral Problem Solving

Most traditional textbooks include sections on problem solving, usually presenting a five- or six-step approach to solving these "problems." Supplementary materials on problem solving present similar approaches and strategies. Unfortunately, most of this material is still grounded in the old "behavioral" approach to learning. These lessons teach the strategies their creators feel are necessary to solve problems, they have the students practice these strategies, and they test to see whether the students have mastered them.

I've seen materials that present a strategy, say guess and check, and then show examples of problems that have been solved using that strategy. The students are then asked to practice using that same strategy on a number of contrived problems. Students who see another way to solve the problem are nevertheless required to use the strategy being "taught" in that lesson.

This is a classic approach to teaching a skill. But problem solving is not a skill; it is a process, a way of thinking. It involves much more than a set of strategies that can be called on and applied as needed.

I also think it's unwise to ask students to practice a single strategy on a given set of problems. Students need to have at their disposal a number of different strategies for solving problems, and of course they need to practice applying these strategies in problem-solving situations.

But if *we* give them the strategies and set up problems for which *we* feel the strategies are best used, then we rob them of the essence of problem solving—thinking and analyzing and trying out ideas. Current researchers say that the pattern-seeking act of sorting through random, illogical, even chaotic input allows the learner to construct knowledge and build on previous learning.

I therefore advocate giving students good problems to solve in an environment that values problem solving, supports risk taking, and provides peer-group models of good problem-solving strategies. That way, the strategies the students learn are their own; as they use them, they own them. They aren't just something memorized out of a book in order to pass a test.

Beginnings

I started using Problems of the Week as extra credit for students who had finished their regular work or wanted a greater challenge. The rest of my program was still rather heavily weighted toward skill acquisition. (The students were grouped into five levels based on their computational ability, a fairly common grouping practice in middle schools at that time.) The problems I chose were not like typical word problems found in a textbook. I felt these wouldn't be a challenge for the students, since we had already "covered" that kind of problem. Instead, I used nonroutine problems drawn from a variety of sources, mainly books of "brain teasers." I set up a section on the bulletin board labeled "Problem of the Week," putting up a new problem every Monday. After the first couple of weeks, I stopped calling attention to the problem. It was there for anyone to try. At first, students had only to give the correct answer in order to get credit for solving the problem. But in talking with them I found they were eager to share the methods they had used to find the answer, and since I was becoming more interested in the process component as well, I began requiring that they write up complete solutions.

Initially, only a small percentage of students attempted the Problems of the Week. They were the highly motivated students who wanted to get as many points as possible in the class, or they were students who were on the borderline between two grades and needed every point they could get, or they were students who just wanted to impress me. But some of their solutions were so good, so well thought out, that I had to share them with the rest of the class. This created a new interest in that small section of the bulletin board, and more students began to try the Problems of the Week.

A Strategical Error

Near the end of the year, I decided that the experience was too valuable for anyone to miss, so I announced that *all* students would be *required* to do the Problems of the Week. This was a major mistake. It was too late in the year, and the procedure had been in place too long as an option. Creating a new requirement at that point was an error in judgment I had difficulty overcoming. But the students—at least most of them—did do the problems, and many of them actually enjoyed them. (Although they couldn't admit that after all the moaning they did when I announced the change.)

In retrospect, I realize that I could have started off the next year with the "required" policy and my students wouldn't have thought much about it. They may not have liked it (after all, it meant more work), but they wouldn't have resisted it to the extent the original class did. This was an important lesson for me, one I have kept in mind over the years as I've implemented new ideas into my teaching. Change is difficult to accept for all of us—teachers, administrators, school boards, and especially students. We should always be aware of the effect any change may have on student attitudes and try to pave the way for change in a nonthreatening way. Sometimes, even though change is necessary, we have to back off and wait for the right opportunity.

Every year since, Problems of the Week have been a required part of my class. The formats for presenting the solution have changed over the years, as have my scoring rubrics, but I am comfortable with the system as it has evolved, and as I said, I have never done anything more exciting or rewarding.

POW Format

Problems of the Week (POWs) are an integral part of my math program, so much so that I can't imagine teaching math without them. I use the acronym POW rather than the abbreviation P.O.W. because the latter, with its connotation of "prisoner of war," may make some students uncomfortable; also, the acronym suggests mathematical POWer! In a nutshell, the idea is to encourage students to solve nonroutine problems on a regular basis, support their attempts to do so, and ask them to communicate their solutions, usually in written form.

When I began, I introduced the POWs early in the year and required that a new one be solved each week. I used a minimal amount of class time for them, just a few minutes to present and clarify the problem and then about half a class period a week later for student presentations. The presentations were strictly voluntary, but I often encouraged students with particularly interesting or elegant solutions to share them. I introduced a new POW each Monday, and the students had until the following Monday to complete their write-ups. I scored the papers on Monday night and returned them on Tuesday, when we discussed the solutions.

I did this for two years, one year having the class do a total of twenty-six POWs. The major drawback to this system was the amount of time it took to score the papers on Monday evenings. The year I used POWs in all of my seventh-grade classes, this meant reading and scoring ninety or more papers every Monday. Even with the relatively simple scoring system I use, this took several hours, time I often needed for lesson planning.

My present plan allows the students five to seven days to complete their POWs, with write-ups always due on a Friday. This gives me the weekend to read and score the papers, and I return them on Monday. Presentations are made, and the POW discussed, on Tuesday. I've also made a modification in the manner in which I present POWs during the year. In order to explain the change, I first need to tell you about Problems of the Day, or PODs.

Problems of the Day

I started using PODs (pronounced as in pea pods) soon after I began requiring students to do POWs. I came across a number of good problems that didn't have the scope or complexity to justify an entire week of problem solving, and not wanting to waste them, I decided to use them in a slightly different format. (My students call short, easy PODs "P-PODs," their shorthand for "Puny PODs.") A Problem of the Day usually became the lesson for that day. The main differences between PODs and POWs were the size of the problem, the time allowed (one day versus one week), the amount of class time devoted to the solution (one whole period versus a few minutes), and the provision for student interaction (required versus permitted). The POD format was typically as follows:

1. **Presentation of the problem.** I handed out the problem in written form or presented it orally. I read the problem clearly once or twice, with emphasis if necessary.
2. **Clarification questions.** Students asked questions about elements of the problem. (No questions about the actual answer or possible solution methods were allowed, however.)

3. **Small-group brainstorming.** In groups of four, students were given a few minutes (time varied depending on the problem and the students) to clarify their understanding of the problem and discuss possible solution strategies.
4. **Large-group questions.** Students had a final opportunity to ask clarification questions or request additional information if needed.
5. **Small-group problem solving.** Students worked together in their groups of four, sharing strategies and ideas. This took most of the class period.
6. **Individual POD write-ups.** Individual students, using the ideas generated in the group problem-solving discussion, completed a four-part write-up about the POD. Although some students were able to begin this part of the process during class time, it was usually completed at home as that night's homework assignment.
7. **Large-group presentations.** Solutions were shared and discussed after the papers were returned.

If a class has a wide range of abilities and limited problem-solving experience, I start the year with PODs. In fact, we do only PODs for the first quarter. This structure allows all students to be successful in their first major problem-solving experiences. Since most of the work in actually solving the problem is done collaboratively in groups during the class period, each student leaves class with a feeling of accomplishment. Their assignment to write up their solution is less daunting with the solution already in hand. Their write-ups highlight individual parts of the overall POW write-up that will be required later in the year. For example, on the first POD, they are asked to write only their process and their answer. Later PODs emphasize their planning and their problem statements. After the first quarter, we do a POW on an average of every other week. Occasionally a POW may relate to the material we are studying. A discount POW or a sales tax POW, for example, could follow a discussion of percentages; or a POW could be correlated with a short story or novel the students are reading in their English class.

Trivia Facts
Many of my POD questions came from problems I found in books or heard from colleagues, but some of them were based on trivia. A colleague and I started using trivia facts during a summer school class in the early 1970s. We did it as a joke, since most kids get asked by their parents, "What did you learn in school today?" and the typical response is, "Nothing." We decided to give our students a clever way to respond

to their parents' inevitable question. Each day, we told them some obscure or arcane bit of information they would then be able to relate to their parents that evening. It was a great diversion, which we continued throughout the summer, and the parents as well as the students enjoyed it. In fact, by the end of the session, students began to contribute the trivia facts themselves.

I forgot about trivia facts until six years ago, when I bought an electronic signboard for my classroom. (I'm sure you've seen similar ones in retail stores and banks.) It's about thirty inches long by four inches tall, and it displays messages with hundreds of small lights. The messages move across the board from right to left. The board is mounted at the front of my classroom, and I use it to make announcements and to recognize the achievements of my students. It's one of the best ways of motivating students I've found: even though students seem to take it for granted after several weeks, they always read it, especially when their names are on it.

Each day's message begins with the date and frequently gives due dates for various assignments, POWs, and projects. I've also used quotes of the day, most of them related to school and learning. One day, I decided to put up a trivia fact just for fun. When students asked about it, I told them it was just something they could use to answer their parents' question about what they had learned.

Then a student asked me that most hated of all questions, "Do we have to know this for a test?" I thought I had permanently erased this question from my students' minds when, at the beginning of the school year, I announced that *everything* we said or did in class was important for them to know, that they should *never* ask whether they needed to know something. I responded in my most patient and understanding voice that *of course* they needed to know it, *of course* it would be on a test. I also told them that since they were allowed to use their notebooks on tests, they wouldn't have to memorize the trivia facts. But they would need to be able to access them.

This put me in a bind, since I had originally intended the trivia facts just for fun. To cover for my hasty response, I began to use trivia with mathematical connotations, facts like *12% of Americans are left-handed* or *The average wooden pencil can draw a line 35 miles long* or *The tip of the minute hand of the Big Ben clock in London travels 146 miles every year.* And instead of asking students merely to restate the trivia facts they had dutifully copied in their notebooks, I asked questions based on these facts. For example, I might ask, *If our school has 825 students, how many of them would you expect to be lefties?* or *How many pencils would*

Most of the questions required fairly straightforward applications of mathematical processes. But some were more complicated. For example, the first real problem-solving activity based on a trivia fact involved the Big Ben statistic: *If Big Ben's minute hand travels 146 miles in a year, how long is the minute hand?* We worked on the problem in class and later verified our answer by looking it up in a reference book. (This, by the way, is one of a number of problems I have given to students without knowing the answer ahead of time. I knew that we could find and verify the answer without difficulty, however. I would never give students a problem unless I was confident that they could find the answer.) From then on, trivia facts often turned into PODs.

The Pencil POD

One of my most successful PODs was one that followed a unit we had just completed on circles and measurement. We had measured dozens of circles and had discovered π and its relationship to a circle's area and circumference; we had developed the formulas for area and circumference; we had written essays about circles. I thought these students really understood circles. The POD was a straightforward application: *How many pencils would you need to draw a line around the world?* We followed the standard POD format:

1. I read the problem to the class, emphasizing the "How many pencils *would you need*" part.
2. Individual students asked clarification questions like "Are these supposed to be new wooden pencils?"
3. I gave the class three or four minutes to brainstorm solutions to the problem. They needed to determine what additional information they would need in order to solve the problem.
4. Individual groups were given one last opportunity to ask questions, up to three questions per group. (When I first started using PODs, I allowed the entire class to ask three questions, but I found this removed the incentive for each group to concentrate on the brainstorming step. They could begin thinking about the solution, confident that some other group would request the information they would need.) Questions included "Where will this line be drawn?" and "What about mountains and rivers and oceans?" and "How far is it around the earth?" My responses were, "Around the equator," "Let's assume that the earth is perfectly flat and that your pencil can

write on any surface, including water, just as it does on paper," and "I can't tell you that. You'll have to rephrase the question." When they complained that I said they could ask any three questions, I reminded them that I didn't say I would necessarily *answer* any three questions. They soon realized they would need to get the information from me in a way that demonstrated their understanding of circles. When they finally asked the diameter (or the radius) of the earth at the equator, I told them. Some groups wasted one or two of their opportunities with questions like "How long a line can a pencil draw?" I simply repeated the trivia fact and reminded them that they could ask only two more questions.

5. Students worked for the rest of the period in their groups, discussing the solution to the problem and, in some cases, starting their POD write-ups.

6. The PODs were turned in the next day. I read and scored them that night and returned them the following day.

7. After getting their papers back, students volunteered to share their solutions. In this case, the students debated whether the answer was 711 or 712 pencils, since the actual numerical answer their calculators had given them was 711.17. This turned out to be an excellent discussion. Some students remembered that I had emphasized the part of the question that said "How many pencils *would you need*." They were able to convince the class that 711 pencils would not be enough to draw a line around the world, thus letting the class see that rounding is used in different ways depending on the situation.

The Ice Cream Pod

Appendix 3–A contains an example of a POD in the format I usually provide to my students. It was given to a seventh-grade class early in the school year (October). The student write-up that follows it is excellent. Outstanding work like this early in the year sets a high standard and greatly improves the quality of everyone's work as the year progresses.

More POD Ideas

Here are some additional PODs I have used with my classes. Some of them came from trivia facts, some came directly from topics we were studying, others were inspired by the wonderful book *Innumeracy,* by John Allen Paulos, in which he describes the consequences of mathematical illiteracy. I followed the same format described previously, and the results were excellent: students got involved with the problems and the mathematics needed to solve them; they discussed mathematics and problem solving with their peers, sometimes quite heatedly; and they communicated their solutions in written form.

- **Beans! Beans! Beans!** How many beans laid end to end would be needed to stretch from the school to the nearest mall? (This POD led to an interesting discussion about measurement: What is the best way to find the length of a single bean? Does it matter which side of the classroom we start from?)
- **Weighty Issue** How much weight would the average American gain in a year with no more than moderate exercise?
- **Water, Water, Everywhere** How many bathtubs would be needed to hold all the water used by this class in a week?
- **Bloody World** How large a cube would be needed to hold all the human blood in the world?
- **Pizza Gluttony** How many acres of pizza are consumed in the United States each year?
- **Diagonal Count** How many diagonals does a polygon have? (This POD, used in an algebra class, resulted in six different algebraic expressions being proposed as answers. Each group was sure that its answer was correct and was able to justify it in terms of the problem. Showing that all six expressions were equivalent was a separate problem offered for extra credit.)

Problems of the Week
POWs differ from PODs in that they have a larger scope. Because students are given an entire week to solve the POW, the problem can be more complex and can involve a variety of strategies and solutions. After students are familiar with solving nonroutine problems, I present POWs like I do PODs with the exception that I don't usually allot as much time for group work. I want students be become more self-reliant in their problem solving. They are still allowed to get help from parents, friends, and teachers if they need it, especially early in the year, but one of my goals is for them to learn persistence and independence in their problem solving, so I encourage them to try to solve the POWs on their own. Some students become independent more quickly than others, but I continue to remind them that solving POWs on their own is a goal to which they should aspire.

I've found that students respond much more enthusiastically when the problems include familiar names, events, and anecdotes. I often include student names in the PODs and POWs, and I try to relate the problems to things that are part of their lives. Often, I include a bit of humor. For example, in a POW called "Cutting the Cheese," the principal characters are four sisters whose last name is Mahj (the four Mahj sisters, a play on the French word for cheese, *fromage*). In the "Cycling" POW, two bicycle shop owners, Wilbur and Orville, have a friend named Kitty help them take an inventory of their cycles. As an aside, the students are asked whether they can guess Kitty's last name. Most of them make the association between Orville and Wilbur Wright, bicycle shop owners and aviators, and Kitty *Hawk,* the site of the Wright brothers' first flight.

Students are asked to write up their solutions to POWs using a specific format. The POW writing guidelines are described below just as they appear at the top of every POW problem (Figure 3–1 is an example):

1. **Problem Statement:** Write a concise statement of the problem. Write clearly enough so that someone picking up your paper could understand exactly what you were asked to do.
2. **Plan:** Tell what you did to *prepare* to solve the problem. How did the problem seem to you when you first read it? Consider what you are asked to find, what you know, what you need to know, and what strategies you can use. Is this problem like any others you've done? Before you begin to work on the problem, make a *guess* at the answer to the problem.
3. **Work:** Explain *in detail* what you did to solve the problem. Use charts and graphs where appropriate. Tell what worked, what didn't work, and what you did when you got stuck. Did you get help from anyone? What kind of help?
4. **Answer:** State your answer(s) to the problem. Does the answer make sense? Could there be other correct answers? Compare your final answer with your original guess. What did you learn from this problem that could help you to solve other problems?

I require the problem statement in order to make sure the students really understand the problem. By restating it, they begin to "own" the problem. I ask students to personalize the problem to create an even stronger identification with its context. In the past, I've made a point of this by having students share particularly creative problem statements with the rest of the class. The result was unexpected: *many* students started writing long (as many as five pages), elaborately detailed problem statements. They would turn the problem into a short story, with the solution becoming the story's resolution. Although I loved their creativity, these "stories" took too long to read. I couldn't skim them

MATH 7 π ZOOLOGY POW

For this problem, provide the following:

I. PROBLEM STATEMENT
Write a concise statement of the problem. Write clearly enough so that someone picking up your paper could understand exactly what you were asked to do.

II. PLAN
Tell what you did to prepare to solve the problem. How did the problem seem to you when you first read it? Consider what you are asked to find, what you know, what you need to know, and what strategies you can use. Is this problem like any others you've done? Before you begin to work on the problem, make a guess at the answer to the problem.

III. WORK
Explain in detail what you did to solve the problem. Use charts and graphs where appropriate. Tell what worked, what didn't work, and what you did when you got stuck. Did you get help from anyone? What kind of help?

IV. ANSWER
State your answer(s) to the problem. Does the answer make sense? Could there be other correct answers? Compare your final answer with your original guess. What did you learn from this problem that could help you to solve other problems?

SAFFRON AND ARISTOTLE'S PROBLEM

You now know about the famous Wright brothers, Orville and Wilbur, and the not-so-famous Wright brothers, Meir and Oscar. Few people realize that there was actually another pair of Wright brothers named Saffron and Aristotle. This pair of brothers owned a small zoo, so small that it contained only three kinds of animals, platypuses, ducks, and spiders.

One day Saffron (Saf) and Aristotle (Ari) decided to take an inventory of the ducks in their zoo. They had heard about all the problems their brothers had experienced with inventories, so they came up with a foolproof plan. Since they only needed to find out how many ducks they had, they each agreed to count two things. They figured that if they each counted two things, at least one of the things would be the number of ducks. Unfortunately, they were just as creative as their other brothers. Saf counted legs and wings and Ari counted bills and wings. They couldn't believe it! Neither of them had simply counted ducks!

They did find that the number of legs minus four times the number of bills was the same as the number of wings. They were just about to take another inventory when their friend, Fawn A. came by and told them that they could determine the number of ducks from the information they already had. She also told them that if one of the spiders were missing a leg, the total number of spider legs would be the same as her math teacher's favorite number. (Her math teacher was Mr. Tsuruda.)

Please help Saf and Ari figure out how many ducks they have in their zoo. And, if you can, explain the significance of each person's name.

FIGURE 3–1

as I usually do when I score POWs. So I decided to stop highlighting problem statements when we shared solutions. Gradually the number of lengthy problem narratives decreased, although I still get a few each week from students who just love to write and create. (They're a pleasure to read, and I often have to remind myself *not* to share them with the rest of the class.)

The planning section is a prompt to get the students to organize their thinking about the problem. It's relatively open-ended, but it helps the students focus on a plan for solving the problem.

The heart of the POW write-up is the work section. Here, the students detail their solution to the problem. I differentiate between the terms *solution* and *answer*. The solution is a presentation of the entire problem-solving process leading to the answer. The purpose of this detailed description is to get the students to reflect on their own problem solving, to analyze the process they used to come up with an answer. This metacognition will help them in future problem-solving situations, and I think it's critical to all learning. We need to build in ways to have students examine their own thinking; it's a critical aspect of helping them construct knowledge.

The final section is more than a simple recording of the answer. It's an analysis of the answer. Or answers. Many POWs have more than one answer, so this is a reminder to students not to stop too soon. In the past, in an attempt to encourage students to consider the reasonableness of their answer and their solution, I have asked them to tell me how they know their answer is right. Students usually wrote banal statements like "I know I'm right because I worked really hard on the problem" or "I know I'm right because my friend got the same answer I did." You can see why I changed "What makes you think your answer is right?" to "Does the answer make sense?" The "What did you learn" question is a continuation of the metacognition I want them to achieve with regard to problem solving. At one time, I had an entire write-up section headed "Learning" in which I asked students to identify what they had learned in solving the POW. The responses tended to be trite and uninspired despite my best efforts to get students to think about their learning, so I decided to eliminate it as a separate section.

I also ask the students to put a cover on their POW, a plain sheet of paper with a graphic illustration of the POW and/or their solution. On the cover, they are to include their name, the date, the amount of time spent on the POW from start to finish, and their personal rating of the POW's level of difficulty from one (easy) to ten (hard). The covers are one more way to encourage creativity and have fun. Figure 3–2 is a student cover for the POW shown in Figure 3–1. Notice the artwork and the creativity, especially the way this student has shown the POW's level of difficulty and the time she spent on it.

A Scoring Rubric

The evaluation criteria I use for POWs and PODs haven't changed much over the years, although the point value for a correct answer has varied. I use these criteria as a quick and easy method of evaluating a POW write-up and communicating that evaluation to the student. We discuss the criteria in detail before the first POD is done and review them with each POD or POW throughout the year. I put the guidelines up on a wall of my classroom in poster form (see Figure 3–3).

When a student gets a paper back, the score is written at the top in this form: 2 + 1 + 5%. In this example, the student received the maximum number of points for the method used to solve the problem, one of two possible points for presentation (because the paper was either sloppy in appearance or unclear in describing the solution), and a 5 percent bonus for getting the correct answer. The three numbers tell students how they did in each area and are convertible to a percentage. In the example above, the score is three out of a possible four (or 75 percent) plus the 5 percent bonus, for a total of 80 percent.

In the past, I've given a full point for the correct answer, still counting it as a bonus, but the resulting five out of four became a very high 125 percent. This undermined my reason for making the correct answer a bonus, which was to eliminate getting the correct answer as the goal. When the answer was worth 25 percent, it *did* become the goal of the problem-solving process.

Our educational system has conditioned students to think of correct answers as the primary objective of mathematics. A skill-oriented curriculum rewards students for determining the one right answer. The POW process attempts to break down this misconception by having students look for more than one answer and asking them to focus on the process and presentation of their solutions instead of on the answer. By making the answer a 5 percent bonus, I tell my students that the answer is important; finding an answer is, after all, the reason we attempt to solve problems. But the point values reflect my belief that the focus in learning to solve problems should be on the *process* of solving problems and the ability to *communicate* that process.

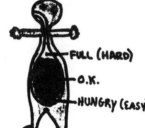

FIGURE 3–2

POW EVALUATION CRITERIA

$$2 \quad + \quad 2 \quad + \quad 5\% \quad \frac{4}{4} \; + \; 5\%$$

process   presentation   answer

PROCESS

0:    Unclear method, or method that would not lead to a
      correct solution.

1:    Method that *could* lead to a correct solution but that
      contains flaws or false assumptions.

2:    Clear, thoughtful method that could lead to a correct
      solution.

PRESENTATION

0:    Unclear, incomplete, sloppy description of problem,
      plan, work, and answer.

1:    Clear description in some areas but not others.
      Sloppy or careless presentation of solution.

2:    Easily understood, neat, well-organized description
      of problem, plan, work, and answer.

ANSWER

0:    Incorrect/incomplete answer.

+ 5%: Correct answer

FIGURE 3–3

Good POWs

What makes a good POW? There are a number of features I look for. First, obviously, it must be within the range of the problem-solving capabilities of my students. It isn't enough for the best students to be able to solve it or even for most of the students to be able to solve it. *All* the students in the class must be capable of solving the problem, although some may require more assistance than others. This criterion is especially important when dealing with a heterogeneously grouped class with a wide range of abilities. The good things about problem solving are that it is easily learned and that improvement is rapid within the right context. Problems that would have been much too difficult early in the school year become excellent POWs as the year and the problem-solving abilities of the students progress.

A POW should also have multiple entry and exit points. That is, it should accommodate a wide range of students. Even though the POW process should not exclude students of lesser ability, it should nevertheless still challenge the better problem solvers. These students will not learn if the problem is too easy, so a POW should be able to be interpreted on a number of levels of difficulty or should contain built-in extensions that will challenge everyone.

Problems that have only one answer and only one way of arriving at that answer tend to be rather uninteresting. I prefer problems with multiple methods and solutions. These problems make the best POWs and lead to the best discussions. I can be fooled by problems because of the limits of my own background. A case in point is "Fleas, Ticks, and Wombats," a POW about wombats with parasite problems: some of the wombats have fleas, some have ticks, and some have both. The clues in the problem allow the student to determine the number of wombats in each category. When I first used this problem several years ago, the class had recently done some work with Venn diagrams. Since the problem is a classic Venn diagram problem, I intended it as a review, expecting that all ninety students would use Venn diagrams in their solutions. Much to my surprise, there were eight different methods used to solve the problem, and Venn diagrams were only the third most popular. One of the alternative methods was much more straightforward and logical than using a Venn diagram.

This experience reinforces two important points: (1) our students do not simply learn a subset of what we tell them and (2) good problem solving is not bound by the conventions of learned strategies. For these reasons, I am wary of choosing POWs that correlate too specifically with the material we are studying in class. With few exceptions, I select

PODs and POWs because they are good problems and I try to sequence them by their level of difficulty and the degree of abstraction necessary to solve them. Students will find ways to use the mathematical understanding they have constructed in their solutions as they deem appropriate; they won't make the same connections we make because their understanding is their own and cannot be forced to match ours at any given time.

The final essential characteristic for a good POW is its ability to engage the students. Students need to find a way of "buying into" the problem. I don't mean that the problem must relate to the real world of the students; some of the best POWs are fanciful, even silly. But the students must be drawn into the problem. They must want to find the solution. Having the students restate the problem is one way to achieve engagement, as is including student names. Sometimes engagement is achieved by the way the problem is presented by the teacher. In each classroom, the relationship between teacher and students is different, and teachers can capitalize on a good relationship by encouraging students to get involved in the problem-solving process.

Sample POWs

Appendixes 3–B and 3–C are examples of successful POWs I have used. The POW in Appendix 3–C is one of the best I've used for students at the seventh- and eighth-grade level, especially if they've had some experience with solving equations. I gave this POW to my seventh-grade prealgebra class before they did work with solving equations and also to my algebra class just after they had learned how to solve simultaneous linear equations. The eighth graders thought the problem was very difficult, giving it an average rating of eight out of ten (ten being the hardest). Most of them tried to use systems of equations and ran into difficulty because they had too many variables and not enough equations. The seventh graders, not bound by algebraic "constraints" found a couple of elegant methods of solving the problem that didn't involve equations at all. Appendix 3–C contains an example of one of those methods.

The student work I've included is the kind all students are capable of doing. When I share work like this with teachers, they often say, "Oh, my students could never do anything like that." Before I started using POWs as part of my math program, I would have had the same reaction. I am continually amazed at and delighted by the work my students do on POWs. Although I've used some of the better POWs for years, I always learn something new from each class that solves them.

Don't be too impressed by the quality of these samples. They are examples of good work, but that work can be replicated or surpassed by your own middle school students.

Time and Difficulty Ratings

I ask my students to include time spent and difficulty ratings on their POW covers not simply to encourage them to reflect on the problem-solving process but because it gives me valuable information about the problem and the class. The amount of time spent is a gauge of the effort the class put into the problem. If some students spend only one hour on the problem, while the class average is four hours, and a few students take as long as six hours, the one-hour students begin to see that problem solving is not necessarily something done in a single session; they learn that patience and persistence are important qualities. I have found without exception that each class spends more time on POWs as the year progresses and each student becomes better at solving problems and communicating about mathematics. It's amazing to me how much progress students make in an area that is at first so difficult for them.

The difficulty ratings of POWs are much higher at the beginning of the year than at the end, even though the problems, in my estimation, are more difficult at the end of the year. The difficulty rating is especially important when using a new POW. Sometimes I assume a problem is easy only to find that it gives the students major difficulties. I always work any new POW myself or try it with a few students before assigning it to the entire class. Once or twice, I've been fooled into thinking I could do a problem easily only to find out during the week that it was much more difficult: in the meantime, the entire class was struggling with the problem.

On the other hand, I've given problems that I thought were difficult and my students have breezed through them. A good example is a POW titled "Bobo and the Time Bomb" (see Figure 3–4). The idea for it came from a parent who sent it to me to illustrate an application of an infinite series. I worked the problem myself using an algebraic method. I shortened the problem somewhat for the POW but offered it in its entirety as an optional extension.

During the week, I kept asking the class how they were doing; I was worried that none of them would get it. I offered to give a hint if anyone needed it, but a few students announced that they had already solved the problem and that it was easy! I couldn't believe it. How could they think this problem was easy? Obviously, they had misinterpreted it. I carefully explained the problem again; they assured me they under-

THE TIME BOMB POW

For this problem, provide the following:

I. PROBLEM STATEMENT
Write a concise statement of the problem. Write clearly enough so that someone picking up your paper could understand exactly what you were asked to do.

II. PLAN
Tell what you did to prepare to solve the problem. How did the problem seem to you when you first read it? Consider what you are asked to find, what you know, what you need to know, and what strategies you can use. Is this problem like any others you've done? Before you begin to work on the problem, make a guess at the answer to the problem.

III. WORK
Explain in detail what you did to solve the problem. Use charts and graphs where appropriate. Tell what worked, what didn't work, and what you did when you got stuck. Did you get help from anyone? What kind of help?

IV. ANSWER
State your answer(s) to the problem. Does the answer make sense? Could there be other correct answers? Compare your final answer with your original guess. What did you learn from this problem that could help you to solve other problems?

BOBO AND THE TIME BOMB

After Bobo successfully completed his hemispheric fencing project, he decided to go on a vacation to get some much-deserved rest and relaxation. He flew down to the Bahamas and was lying on the beach catching a few rays when his good friend, Bozo came running up to him. He explained that Bobo was in grave danger because of the fence he had built. It seems that some very powerful drug lords were upset because the fence was interfering with their drug trafficking. They had vowed to kill Bobo with a bomb.

Bobo ran to his hotel room, locked himself in, and tried to figure out what to do. He noticed that the alarm clock had some funny wires coming out of it and a strange package was concealed below the nightstand. That was it! But he was locked in the room. He frantically looked around for a way out when he saw the note taped to the window.

The note told him that if he could solve a certain problem, he could disable the bomb and save his life. The problem was to determine the EXACT time when the minute hand and the hour hand of the clock would be in the same position. Of course this is a fairly common occurrence; it happens 22 times every day starting at 12:00:00.00 (12 o'clock midnight, zero minutes, zero seconds, zero hundredths of a second).

The clock read 2:15, so Bobo knew that he had only about an hour to find the next time the hands would coincide or he would be history. Bobo solved the problem in less than an hour. Your task is to solve the same problem, but you have to find all 22 times and explain your solution. Good luck!

FIGURE 3–4

stood. Soon, other students reported that they had completed the POW and that it was easy.

I was never more eager to read the POWs than I was that week. It turned out that the students had seen a simple, elegant way of approaching the problem that involved nothing more than an arithmetic calculation. The average difficulty rating for this POW was only a five, and the average time spent was only two hours. Most students went on to do the optional extension and got the correct answer.

Sharing Session

A typical POW sharing session begins with an overview of the problem and some general comments from me. I usually take notes as I score the papers, noting trends, the number of different strategies used, the time spent, and the difficulty ratings. Often I find that several students are skipping steps or omitting diagrams or jumping to conclusions. I go over these types of comments with the entire class; if I had to write the same comments on each student's paper, my evaluations would take twice as long. Students are always amazed by the number of different strategies used, especially at the beginning of the year when they each come up with only one. Hearing that five different methods were used previews the sharing session and creates curiosity about how other students did the problem. We also discuss different strategies and recognize elegant solutions as opposed to those that are done by brute force or number crunching. These terms become very much a part of the students' vocabulary as the year progresses.

I always take class time to recognize those students who did an exceptional job on the POW. Often these are the students whose papers are posted on the "Outstanding POWs" section of the bulletin board, but there are frequently more good POWs than there is room on the board. It has become an honor for students to have their papers chosen as outstanding POWs. I try to pick papers that illustrate some of the points I want to make about problem solving and communication, such as concise problem statements, effective use of graphs, unique methods of solution. I also try to select POWs of students who have shown improvement or who have previously had to struggle with them. Students are encouraged to look at the posted POWs, to take them down and go over them in detail, even to take them home and study them. This increases the recognition given to the students whose papers are on display and provides a real model for students who need help.

The heart of the sharing session involves student presentations. I ask for volunteers to present parts of their solutions, and I never have fewer than three volunteers. Usually, after a few students have made their presentations, others will add to what an original presenter has said. I tell the students that I would like each of them to share before the end of the year, but I've never had a class in which this has actually happened. Most of the students do share, but some lack the confidence to speak to a large group.

I never force a shy or an unsure student to get up in front of the class. These students contribute and share in their small groups, and it's cruel and counterproductive to embarrass them. I will say that students who I thought would never volunteer sometimes surprise me. For one of them to raise a hand is a major breakthrough, and I have to mask my surprise and elation. I think the safe environment I try to create helps them take the risk. I was a shy student and hated to be called on, so I identify with what these students are experiencing.

Students may use transparencies and the overhead projector to help illustrate their presentations, and the other students are generally very good about paying attention. I ask the class to take notes so that they will be able to apply the other methods they learn to future POWs. I limit the time of each presentation and insist that the students get to the heart of their idea quickly, because most students tend to dwell on the details. All told, the POW sharing usually takes no more than twenty or thirty minutes.

POW Presentation

The second number in a POW score refers to presentation: the description of the problem, plan, work, and answer. Students receive lower scores for incomplete or unclear writing and for sloppy papers. Some students come into the class with the attitude that the work is being done for the teacher only and so they don't care how it looks. I'm fairly picky about neatness normally, and with POWs, I'm *especially* strict about the way the final product looks. I tell the students that it makes no sense to spend several hours on a problem and then present it in a sloppy, messy form. I want them to take pride in the work they have done.

In the case of POWs, a messy paper can cost students one of four possible points, or 25 percent of their grade. This may seem a severe penalty for messiness, but it gets the message across. In fact, many students now use computers and word processors to complete their POW write-ups. Neat, well-organized POWs are *much* easier to read, and when I'm scoring ninety or more papers, this can make a huge difference.

I encourage students to present their POWs using alternative formats. I've been given posters, audiocassettes, and even several video-tapes. (In one recent week, I received two audio and nine video POWs from the four classes that were solving the same problem.) The video-tapes usually start with an elaborate reenactment of the problem. The solutions are sometimes acted out as well and are followed up with a visual account of how the student arrived at an answer. I've also begun allowing students to submit a POW with a partner once each quarter.

I'm thinking of discouraging the audio POWs because of the time it takes to listen to them. A student can record an audiocassette in about the same amount of time it takes to write out the POW, but it takes me much longer to listen to the tape than it does to read a write-up. The average POW write-up is about three pages long. I can usually read a single POW and score it in three or four minutes. But the audiotapes I have received are usually about fifteen minutes long. There is no way to skim the tape, so I end up taking a full fifteen minutes or more for each.

I don't plan to discourage video POWs because they are usually so well done and creative. Most of the students who have submitted video POWs put in many hours of production in addition to the time spent actually solving the POW, and I don't want to discourage that kind of motivation and interest. Besides, there have been relatively few of them (so far), and they can be shown to the class as part of the sharing session. Also, some of the videos are perfect examples of good POWs. I have a couple of favorites that I plan to use for years to illustrate aspects of problem solving to future classes.

The "POWnoloply" gameboard in Figure 3–5 was created as part of an open-ended project after the students had done several POWs. Many of the ideas we had discussed throughout the year are included in the game: stop and think about the concept of the problem, reread and try again, don't jump to conclusions, be able to explain your answer, consider more than one right answer, etc.

POW Scoring—The Time Factor

Although it takes a significant amount of time to read and score POWs every week, I feel it's an investment well worth the improvements generated in my students' learning and attitude. A class set for a typical POW takes about an hour and a half to read and score. I usually read POWs from two to four classes in any given week. This is a major block of time, and it doesn't account for the other classes I teach. I try to do POWs in each of my classes, and I try to stagger the due dates so that

FIGURE 3–5

I don't ever have more than three classes to read at once, but it is a burden. It may be the biggest challenge facing math teachers who want to use more writing as part of their instruction. English teachers have faced this problem for years, and perhaps we can look to them for solutions.

One way to avoid the problem is simply to assign fewer POWs. Some English teachers resort to this tactic because of the overwhelming amount of student writing they have to read. One parent told me that his daughter was learning a tremendous amount from the POWs about mathematics *and* about writing. He claimed she did more writing in math than she did in her English class. However, I don't believe that assigning fewer POWs is really a solution, because it unburdens the teacher at the expense of the students. As its name implies, a Problem of the Week should be done every week or nearly every week. Having a problem of the month may be slightly better than nothing, but it just isn't enough. One year, wanting to do as many POWs as possible in all of my classes, I reduced the number I assigned my seventh graders, classes in which I had previously focused heavily on POWs. I saw a sharp decline in their problem-solving abilities. Problem solving improves tremendously through continued application: the more you do it, the better you get.

Another technique some math teachers borrow from English teachers is to make use of the revision process. The theory is that students can learn a great deal about problem solving and about communication by revising their original POW write-ups. Students can be given a POW assignment one week and then be asked to revise it the following week. Reading a revised POW takes significantly less time than reading an original, so a teacher's reading time is reduced. I haven't tried this on a large scale myself. However, I do include revision in the POW sequence in another way. I *require* all students who score less than three out of four to revise their POW and resubmit it, and students with a score of three may revise their POW to get a higher score. I want to teach my students that they don't have to get it right on the first try. In real life, we are often given opportunities to revise original work. In addition, I give all my students a portfolio assignment in which they must revise a POW to make it as close to perfect as possible. (A maximum score does not mean that a POW is perfect.)

A third idea I learned from an English teacher is the concept of response groups. With this method, I give students some of the responsibility for evaluating the work of their peers. After a class has completed a POW, I give their papers to another class that has completed the same POW. We agree on a scoring rubric, and students read the papers in small groups. Each paper is read by at least two students, who each write their score on the back of a tag attached to the paper. If they agree on the score, they are done with the paper for the moment. If they disagree, a third student also reads the paper and the three readers discuss the score. Once the group members agree on a score for each paper the group has been given, they are asked to discuss each paper and write comments to the author. I ask that they write some positive comments regardless of the score.

I've tried response groups twice, and I have been very impressed with the attitudes of the student readers. They take this task very seriously, and their comments are excellent, especially the positive comments on weak papers. When I read three sets of POWs in one evening, I don't have time to make individual comments, so the student feedback is very helpful.

I have, however, found two potential drawbacks to using response groups. First, since the authors of the papers are anonymous to the readers, there is no way to account for individual differences, such as a learning disability. (Some students are not inclined to make this kind of allowance anyway.) As a rule, students are much more strict about grading than I am. Secondly, response groups occupy an additional full day of class time. (This part doesn't bother me, since I feel it is time well spent.)

When I first started experimenting with response groups, I duplicated nine student POW write-ups from a previous year, some very good, some average, and some poor. Right after the class had completed the same POW, I handed out the samples to the groups. We followed this procedure: (1) each student read all nine samples; (2) each student sorted the samples into three groups—best, worst, and in-between; (3) the group discussed the sorting and resolved any differences of opinion; (4) the group brainstormed about the qualities that made the best samples good and the qualities that made the worst samples bad; (5) we shared these brainstormed lists with the whole class, creating a big list of characteristics of good POWs and bad POWs. This method proved amazingly successful. The list the class generated was much better and more meaningful than anything I could have given them. The best part was that it came from them. They saw firsthand what makes up a good POW.

The success of the response group idea is encouraging, and although I believe that the teacher needs to read many of the POWs personally, I definitely plan to use more response groups in the future.

POW Benefits

In addition to the obvious improvement POWs generate in students' abilities to solve problems and communicate about mathematics, they benefit the students' perceptions and attitudes. Many students enter middle school math classes with a sense of foreboding. They fear math because they weren't successful at it in prior grades, and they may feel they are part of that group of students who "just don't get math." It is critically important that we try to turn around these feelings about mathematics. We need to provide a safe environment in which all students have an opportunity to succeed. Granted, some may have to work harder than others to reach certain levels of success, but everyone can succeed.

Watering down the curriculum won't work; success is perceived by the students in terms of their having accomplished a meaningful goal. Getting the answer to an easy drill problem or a simple word problem is unlikely to be meaningful to students, but solving a big Problem of the Week can be. Countless of my students, through anonymous questionnaires or portfolio reflections or informal conversations, have commented that the POWs taught them to think and gave them the confidence to solve any problem.

POWs also help students view mathematics as a complete body of knowledge rather than as a series of individual strands. POWs aren't usually limited to a single strand: instead, they cross strands and illustrate the interconnectedness of the various mathematical topics. This broad vision of mathematics is very important for students, especially middle school students who will soon be making academic and career choices that will affect the rest of their lives.

Parent Involvement

Some teachers are surprised that I encourage parents to work with their children on the POWs. They ask whether I worry that a parent may simply do the work for the child. And this is definitely a concern, especially in a community that places a high value on education. But I find it a relatively minor concern. I'd much rather a parent be too involved than not involved at all, because it's fairly easy to explain the goals of the program to parents who care deeply about their children's success. It isn't difficult to convince them that their "help" can sometimes be counterproductive, especially when we are trying to produce independent problem solvers.

Parent involvement is almost totally positive from my point of view. I want the students to share the POWs with their parents, with their whole families. This is part of an overall responsibility for parent and community education that many of us ignore. Parents can be very supportive if they are informed of the goals of a program and are invited to participate, even if that participation is necessarily limited. I've had numerous parents report that the POWs became a major part of the family's dinner conversation each week. Often, parents will see me outside of school and comment on the current POW or tell me how much they enjoyed a previous POW. And, as with the "Bobo and the Time Bomb" POW I discussed earlier in this chapter, parents sometimes contribute problems to my collection. POWs have become an integral part of the culture of my math classes and have entered the life of students outside of school.

One definition of mathematical power includes the statement that mathematically powerful students possess attitudes of appreciation, confidence, curiosity, inventiveness, persistence, reflection, and willingness. Wouldn't it be great if each of our students could develop these attitudes? Wouldn't it be great if our students could learn to work together toward a common goal? Wouldn't it be great if our students could communicate about mathematics with enthusiasm and interest? I've seen these things happen with a wide range of students over several years. I've seen them in classes that were fairly structured and skill-oriented and in classes that have begun to embrace the spirit of constructivism. I've seen them in classes with textbooks and nightly homework and in classes without texts and with only limited amounts of homework. I've seen them close-up, because each of the classrooms has been my own. POWs have been a big part of the transformation in my teaching. In retrospect, it appears that my approach to POWs has evolved as I have changed my thinking about how students learn; in reality, however, the POWs were a major catalyst in that process of change. Using POWs has made me a better teacher.

Appendix 3–A

ICE CREAM POD

For this problem, provide the following:

I.   PROBLEM STATEMENT
Write a concise statement of the problem. Write clearly enough so that someone picking up your paper could understand exactly what you were asked to do.

II. PLAN
Tell what you did to **prepare** to solve the problem. How did the problem seem to you when you first read it? Consider what you are asked to find, what you know, what you need to know, and what strategies you can use. Is this problem like any others you've done? Before you begin to work on the problem, make a **guess** at the answer to the problem.

III. WORK
Explain **in detail** what you did to solve the problem. Use charts and graphs where appropriate. Tell what worked, what didn't work, and what you did when you got stuck. Did you get help from anyone? What kind of help?

IV. ANSWER
State your answer(s) to the problem. Does the answer make sense? Could there be other correct answers? Compare your final answer with your original guess. What did you learn from this problem that could help you to solve other problems?

The seventh grade class at a certain middle school decided to have an ice cream party to celebrate their outstanding grades. They decided to make ice cream cones. But they were all very independent thinkers, and they each wanted to have a different cone.

Unfortunately, the school was only willing to provide them with two ice cream flavors, vanilla and chocolate. They knew that if they used only single-scoop cones, they could make only two different cones:

They figured out that if they used double-scoop cones, they could make four different cones:

There are 256 students in this outstanding 7th grade class. How many scoops of ice cream would have to be used in each cone in order to make a different cone for each person?

41

I. Problem Statement

The seventh grade class at Jordan Middle School decided to have an ice cream party to celebrate their outstanding grades. They decided to make ice cream cones. But they were all independent thinkers, and they each wanted to have a different cone.

Unfortunately, the school was only willing to provide them with two ice cream flavors, vanilla and chocolate. They knew that if they used only single-scoop cones, they could make only two different cones:

They figured out that if they used double-scoop cones, they could make four different cones:

There are 256 students in this outstanding 7th grade class. How many scoops of ice cream would have to be used in each cone in order to make a different cone for each person?

II. Plan

In order to solve the problem I needed my calculator, pencil, and a scratch piece of paper. When I first read the problem it seemed to me not so hard because I knew how to figure out the answer, but I knew it would take a while to write it up. I knew that I could use a tree diagram or a strategy called Impossible Consecutive Sums (powers of 2) to figure it out.

The Ice Cream POD also reminds me of some problems we did a couple weeks ago. These problems were the tree diagrams and the Paper Folding POD, so I sort of knew how to deal with this problem.

I also thought it would be a good idea to make a guess before I figured out the answer. I did this so I could compare answers at the end. My guess was ██

III. Work

What I did to solve the problem was to first figure out or remind myself what was needed. I needed to find out how many scoops of ice cream were needed to make a different cone for each person. Now that I know what I am to figure out I decided to start off by making a tree diagram......

1.   2.   4.   8. 16. 32.

more on next page→

46

64. 128.

64. 128.

Since I do not have
enough room to show
the last column which
would be 256, I just
decided to tell you. I
also found a pattern
while I was working. The
pattern is...... ~~powers of 2.~~

$1 \times 2 = 2$ $32 \times 2 = 64$
$2 \times 2 = 4$ $64 \times 2 = 128$
$4 \times 2 = 8$ ~~$128 \times 2 = 256$~~
$8 \times 2 = 16$
$16 \times 2 = 32$

→

The tree diagram is one way you can figure it out. The other way is what I showed you before, ~~powers of two~~.....

☒	2
1	2
2	4
4	8
8	16
16	32
32	64
64	128
128	■■■

This pattern is also called ~~powers of two~~, just like the tree diagram!

Both of these strategies worked, but I did get help from Jill. I needed help on the powers of two. This was because I didn't know exactly if we were suposed to make a chart, bar graph, or just exactly how we were suposed to show the powers of two on our write-up. She explained it to me quite well, I thought.

IV. Answer

The answer that I came up with at the end was 8 because when I did the powers of two I got to 256. It took me 8 tries or 8 multiplication problems to get to the answer of 256. So, since it took me 81 times to get to 256, the answer is 8 scoops. The answer makes sense to me because it seems right that you could make 256 combinations each time using 8 scoops.

Now it is time to compare my guess to the real answer, it is a perfect match! I guessed 8, and the real answer is 8! I don't know excatly how this worked out it just did.

I also learned alot from this problem. I learned that with hard work and consentration you can produce something unbeliably succsesful.

THE QUADRATIC PIZZA POW

For this problem, provide the following:

I. PROBLEM STATEMENT

Write a concise statement of the problem. Write clearly enough so that someone picking up your paper could understand exactly what you were asked to do.

II. PLAN

Tell what you did to **prepare** to solve the problem. How did the problem seem to you when you first read it? Consider what you are asked to find, what you know, what you need to know, and what strategies you can use. Is this problem like any others you've done? Before you begin to work on the problem, make a **guess** at the answer to the problem.

III. WORK

Explain **in detail** what you did to solve the problem. Use charts and graphs where appropriate. Tell what worked, what didn't work, and what you did when you got stuck. Did you get help from anyone? What kind of help?

IV. ANSWER

State your answer(s) to the problem. Does the answer make sense? Could there be other correct answers? Compare your final answer with your original guess. What did you learn from this problem that could help you to solve other problems?

BOBO AND THE PIZZA PARTY

After making a fortune with Koko, his trusty camel, Bobo decided to throw a huge party. He wanted to invite all of his friends from desert and the carnival plus all of his fans from the game show and those who supported him in his fence project. This was going to be quite a few people, so he ordered a gigantic pizza, the largest pizza in the world.

The pizza was so big that it was going to cost Bobo a small fortune just to cut it. The World's Largest Pizza Cutting Company charged Bobo $500 per straight cut. Obviously, Bobo was going to have to slice up the pizza in as few cuts as possible in order to save money.

What are the minimum and maximum number of people Bobo can invite to his celebration if he uses 3 cuts? 4 cuts? 5 cuts? 6 cuts? n cuts? Assume that each person at the party gets one piece of pizza.

THE QUADRATIC PIZZA POW
(Better known as "The Pizza Party")
STARRING BOB, SLOB, AND "THE PARTY"

I. Problem Statement

After making a great amount of money in "The Desert" , with a camel he named Slob, and a known quality Swiss army knife, Bob decided to throw away some of his enormous amount of money on a pizza party. He wanted to invite all of his friends from the desert and the carnival, plus all of his fans from the game show, and those who supported him through his fence project, and finally those who watched his amazing run in BOB and THE BRIDGE. This was going to be a gigantic party, so he better get a "large" pizza right? No, but that's what he thought anyway, so he ordered the largest pizza in the world.

Being so big Bob could not cut this pizza alone. The pizza being so big would cost Bob a fortune just to cut it. The World Largest Pizza Company for idiots charged Bob $500 per straight cut. Obviously, for Bob, it would be a good idea to cut the pizza into as few cuts as possible in order to save on his load of money.

What are the minimum and maximum number of people Bob could invite to the party, if he uses 3 cuts? 4 cuts? 5 cuts? 6 cuts? n cuts? Assume that each person at the party gets one piece of the pizza.

II. Plan

I have prepared for the following problem by getting out a piece of scratch paper, a pen and a ruler. When I first read the problem, I considered the problem to be very hard, and considered making sure that I was free for a couple of hours, so I could work on the problem. I know that we must find a pattern and therefore a formula so we could find the solution for n cuts, so what I really needed to find was the formula. Therefore what I need to know is the formula to find the answer to this problem. For this reason I will follow strategies that show the pattern in a way I could find it easily. I don't think this problem is like any others I've done, therefore, I have only the slightest idea of what strategies to follow.

Guess: 2^n (n being the number of the cut) for the maximum and n + 1 for the minimum.

III. Work

The first thing that I tried to do to solve this problem, was to make some pictures where the circle in the picture represents the pizza. I experimented making cuts (shown as the lines going through the circle).

I quickly noticed that to get the minimum number of cuts, Bob has to make sure he never cuts through any of the previous cuts he made inside the pizza (It does not matter if the cuts intersect outside of the pizza):

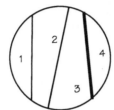

This was easy but how about the maximum ? I started with 2 lines and added a third (the bold line) that does not cross either of the 2 lines. This only gives me 1 additional pizza piece:

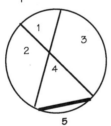

Now I try to cut through at least one of the existing lines. This gives me 2 additional pizza pieces:

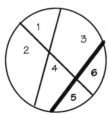

I can do one better and cut through both lines and that gives me 3 more pizza pieces:

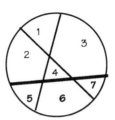

I think I got it. I cannot cut more than the 2 lines I already had. 7 is therefore the maximum for 3 cuts.

Now what is the pattern ? I noticed that the third cut gives me 3 new pizza pieces. I quickly checked if this is true for 4 cuts

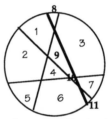

This would indicate cut n that cuts all n-1 cuts results in n new pizza pieces. Let me check if this is also true starting with an uncut pizza.

An uncut pizza has obviously only one piece. The first cut always adds one piece. The second cut:

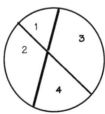

hurrah adds 2 piece.

Let's put all this information in a table to try to find the formula we are so desperately looking for:

# of cuts	Maximum pieces of pizza	Minimum pieces of pizza
0	1	1
1	2	2
2	4	3
3	7	4
4	11	5
n	?	n+1

The formula for the minimum number of pieces is easy: n+1. But the maximum ?

Since the $n^{Th.}$ cut adds n pieces but we start with 1 piece for the uncut pizza, the formula seems to be: 1 + the sum of the numbers from 0 to n. This can be written as:

$$1 + \frac{n\,(n+1)}{2}$$

VI. Conclusion

Since each person would get 1 piece, the number of pieces would equal the number of people that would go to the party. Therefore the minimum number of people coming to the party if Bob paid for 3 cuts is 4, and the maximum is 7. For 4 cuts the minimum would then be 5 and the maximum is 11. Then for 5 cuts the minimum would be 6 and the maximum is 16. And, for 6 cuts the minimum is 7 and the maximum is 22. Finally for n cuts the minimum is n + 1 and the maximum is $\frac{n\,(n+1)}{2}$ + 1. There is obviously 1 answer, that is if **Bob does not eat from the pizza!** If Bob wants to eat a piece of his pizza he will only be able to invite a minimum of n and a maximum of $\frac{n\,(n+1)}{2}$ guests.

My final answer compared to my original guess makes a lot more sense. Conclusion: Always go with the strategies that make most sense.

3–C   Appendix

THE TRAIN POW

For this problem, provide the following:

I.   PROBLEM STATEMENT
Write a concise statement of the problem. Write clearly enough so that someone picking up your paper could understand exactly what you were asked to do.

II.   PLAN
Tell what you did to **prepare** to solve the problem. How did the problem seem to you when you first read it? Consider what you are asked to find, what you know, what you need to know, and what strategies you can use. Is this problem like any others you've done? Before you begin to work on the problem, make a **guess** at the answer to the problem.

III.   WORK
Explain **in detail** what you did to solve the problem. Use charts and graphs where appropriate. Tell what worked, what didn't work, and what you did when you got stuck. Did you get help from anyone? What kind of help?

IV.   ANSWER
State your answer(s) to the problem. Does the answer make sense? Could there be other correct answers? Compare your final answer with your original guess. What did you learn from this problem that could help you to solve other problems?

BOBO AND THE TRAIN

Bobo was walking across a bridge one day. He knew that a train was due to come across that bridge soon, but he thought he could make it. It was a nice sunny day, and there was a great view from the bridge, so Bobo walked very slowly, enjoying the view and savoring the warmth of the spring day.

He was 2/3 of the way across the bridge, when the sound of a train whistle brought him instantly back to reality. A huge locomotive pulling tons of boxcars was coming directly at him at 45 miles per hour! Using all of his powers of mathematical thought and analysis, Bobo immediately figured that he could run directly ahead and get to the far edge of the bridge at the exact same instant as the train. But he also knew that he could run back in the direction from which he had come and get to <u>that</u> end of the bridge at the exact same instant the train overtook him.

How fast does Bobo run?

BOBO POW

I. Problem Statement

Bobo, a runaway clown, was crossing a lovely bridge one day. Being a clown of a decidedly lower IQ, he took his time. He had a feeling that a train would come, but just when he didn't know.

Bobo was 2/3 of the way across when he fell down. His ear hit the rail, and he heard it humming as though a train was coming. Now, even dumb clowns have their moments. Through the magic of Mr. Tsuruda's POWs, Bobo miraculously could compute in his mind how fast this train was coming (45 mph, of course).

He also figured out in the blinking of an eye that if he started running at a certain speed, he would make it, just barely. He also figured (thanks to Mr. Tsuruda again) that if he ran back the other way at the same speed, he would also make it, just barely.

II. Procedure

First I drew a diagram (Diagram I). It showed the bridge. The bridge is three inches long. It is divided into thirds (inches). At the time Bobo is standing at the 2/3 mark. At right is the train, and above the train is the train's speed (45 mph). I tried to do it in steps. We knows that it takes Bobo and the train the same amount of time to get to the end of the bridge.

I wanted to see how Bobo would do the other way. I called the distance of every third of the bridge a. By the time Bobo had reached the 1/3 mark, the train was at the 3/3 mark.

By the time Bobo was at the O/3 mark the train was even with him. We know this is true because in Mr. Tsuruda's write-up it said he would be safe either way.

What this means is that the train could travel 3a in the same time that it took Bobo to travel only a. This means Bobo was running 1/3 as fast as the train (He must have been pretty motivated, because a track star cannot keep up a pace like (a) for a sustained time) This also means that the distance that the train was away from the bridge was equal to the length of the bridge.

I tried to do this on my own by using logic, but it did not work. For the second time in as many POWs, I relied on my mother for guidance. For the first part of our discussion, we both thought it could not be solved. She thought there were some basic factors missing. We thought the length from the train to the bridge was important, and that the length of the bridge was also important. Both were apparently missing. O ye of little faith!

We then looked at it in the way Diagram II illustrates. It all became so clear after that. We came to the conclusions above, and so I sent out to write it up.

I tried four different approaches: logic, mother, a cop out of "There is no answer!", and the correct approach, the formula Bobo = a and the train = 3a.

III. Conclusion

Bobo was running at the speed of 15mph. I think I got it

right because I have checked my answer numerous times. I figured out the speed by taken the train's speed and dividing it by 3 . . . . divided by three is fifteen. God, I'd love to have Bobo on my school's track team.

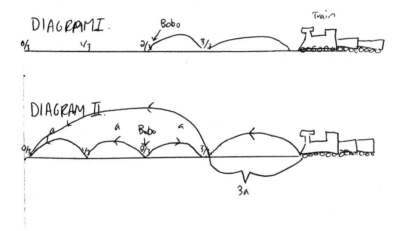

Student Writing 4

I was recently asked to speak at a conference dealing with an interdisciplinary approach to teaching. Although I had been doing some work with an English and a social studies teacher as part of a seventh-grade team, I did not consider the ideas we had tried to be exemplary, nor did I consider myself in any way an expert in this area. I explained this to the conference organizer, who then mentioned the work I had been doing with writing in my math classes. I responded that although I had been using writing in math for several years, I didn't consider this to be interdisciplinary.

I still don't. I feel that writing is a tool for student learning and for teacher assessment, one that doesn't "belong" to any single discipline. I am at a point now where I cannot imagine teaching math without using writing. I feel that student writing in mathematics fulfills three objectives: (1) it allows students to reflect on their own thinking and therefore gain insights into the mathematics they are learning; (2) it teaches students the value of communicating about mathematics; and (3) it provides an excellent means of assessing student learning.

Beginnings

For years, it never occurred to me to have my students write in math class. But as colleagues from other disciplines shared ideas with me, I began to see the value of having students write. At first, I used writing as a way for students to tell me what they understood and didn't understand about particular topics. The feedback they gave me was helpful in planning future instruction, but it also gave me specific insights into the misunderstandings that were occurring.

As I began to use writing more and more in my classes, I found that it provided a window into students' thinking about solving problems. By requiring students to write out their solutions in detail, I learned things about the students and their thought processes that tests had never shown me. I actually saw how they were analyzing problems, in a way I had never before experienced. As I mentioned earlier, the Problem of the Week writing has become a cornerstone of my teaching. In the same way that students' group work encourages students to talk about mathematics and thus serves as a window into the collective thinking of the group or class, student writing is a personal window into the thinking of an individual student.

Essays in Math?

Most students do not like to write. When I announce at the beginning of the year that we will be doing lots of writing in our math class, they groan. And when I assign numerous essays early in the year, they complain, "What is this, an English class? Why do we have to write so many essays?" I explain that writing is another tool for learning, and most of them eventually stop complaining, especially when they find out that no essay ever has a length requirement and that I never check for spelling or grammatical errors. This may be controversial, especially to those who believe that it is every teacher's responsibility to teach writing and that spelling and grammar are part of writing. I do feel that I am teaching writing, but I am doing it within the context of mathematics.

Students seem to improve their ability to write clearly by writing, by examining examples of good writing, and by writing some more. The key, in my opinion, is practice. When I had the time and energy to assign twenty-six Problems of the Week to my seventh-grade classes a few years ago, their abilities to express themselves in written form improved tremendously, much more than the next year, when I assigned only eighteen POWs. If I had corrected each paper for spelling and grammar in addition to reading for a mathematically correct process and clear explanation, I would probably have accomplished two things: I would have turned off many of the students with all my corrections, and I would have burned myself out with the time it would have taken. I doubt that I would have been able to sustain my interest in having students write in mathematics.

At the beginning of the year students ask how long an essay has to be, probably as a result of being given word or page minimums in other classes. I tell them that I am not interested in length, only quality, but that a certain length is necessary in order to achieve quality. For example, if the assignment is to describe what they've learned from a particular class activity, I tell them the essay has to be long enough for them to tell me what they have learned. For some that may be one page, for others, several pages. I stress that I am not interested in "filler," that length does not equal quality. But I also remind them that if they do not succeed in telling me clearly what they learned, I will give the paper back and ask them to rewrite it. Note that I do not simply give them an F and forget about it. I tell them to rewrite the paper for full credit. The reason is simple: I want to find out what they learned from the activity, and I want them to reflect on the activity and think about their learning. Writing is a way to accomplish these goals.

Student reflection is an important part of learning. When learners think about the activity they have just completed and reflect upon the learning they have done, they are engaging in metacognition. The idea isn't new; we've know for years that reviewing and summarizing one's notes is an aid to learning. But seldom have we as teachers built in opportunities for our students to engage in metacognition. Asking students to write about their learning is a way of forcing them to think about what an activity meant to them and what they took away from the experience.

I frequently assign essays as homework. A typical assignment might be titled "What I Learned from Today's Activity." Figure 4–1, an essay written by a sixth grader, illustrates how an open-ended assignment like this can reveal much more than just a mathematical understanding of a concept. This student tells about the pride of accomplishment she felt when her group solved the puzzle, the level of cooperation in her group, and her intention to share the activity with her family. Student excitement like this helps mathematics become part of the culture of a school and a community.

Or I might ask the students to begin an essay *before* an activity and "Predict What Will Happen If. . . ." In this case, the students typically begin the writing assignment in class and then finish it at home. For example, in a probability activity called "Mix or Match," I asked my students to predict what would happen if we mixed two red beans and one blue bean, removed one bean without looking, and then examined the two remaining beans. Would there be more mixes or matches if we did this several times? They began their essay by describing their prediction and their reasoning. We then did the experiment in class and collected class data. After discussing the data, I asked the students to continue their essay by describing what actually happened and why, and then to predict the outcome of the next step in the experiment:

What I Learned From Todays Activity

What I learned from todays activity was how to set up clues. Actually how to set up clues correctly. Usually when I make up a guessing game nobody understands the game. But your clues were wonderful, They told us exactly how to put it together. It was also fun on my part. I also learned how to stack blocks in a very neat way. This activity was my favorite one of all it was really fun. I also learned how to figure out puzzles. All you have to do is read the clues first and kind of get a good idea of the object in your head, then you read one by one and try to put the blocks or anything else in the right place. When you get finished you feel so proud of yourself and your friends for figuring out something really hard out. Sometimes it is not very hard but if it is hard all you have to do is concentrate and read the clues first to yourself. I also learned now to cooperate with other people easier. Because usually I like to do things by myself, but this was really fun for me because nobody argued with eachother and we listened to everybody even though they might have been wright or wrong. Also I learn how to make new mysterie games out of what the clues that you gave us. And I think my family will have a great time with that. And those are the things that I learned on todays really fun project.

FIGURE 4–1

what would happen if we took three red beans and one blue and removed two beans without looking? The whole essay process can continue along with the activity. In the essay shown in Figure 4–2, a student discusses predicted results for the four-blue-one-red stage of this experiment.

It's a good idea to vary the audience for writing assignments. Students write with a completely different style when writing for a different audience. For example, instead of asking my sixth graders to write an essay telling me everything they knew about circles, I had them write letters to fourth graders explaining the mysterious world of circles. The letters they wrote (see the example in Figure 4–3) were interesting, humorous, and revealing. Not only were they more fun to read than essays written when the students knew I would be the only audience, but they were more informative about the students' knowledge of circles than any test could be. In addition, with the cooperation of a principal and teachers at an area elementary school, the letters were actually used in fourth-grade classrooms.

In my present school, I had my seventh graders write letters to sixth graders. One of the sixth-grade teachers had her students read the letters in groups, summarize the learning, and then write personal letters back to my students. My students learned a great deal from the process of writing the letters, I learned about their understanding of the concepts from reading the letters, the sixth graders learned about a new concept, and the seventh graders were thrilled to receive letters back complimenting them on how helpful their letters were. It was a wonderful activity, one I have repeated several times with similar results.

At the beginning of the year, most students need some structured directions or prompts in order to write clear essays. I used to have students write an essay about their first quiz after they received the results. These results were generally not as good as most students expected, because the test was unlike any of the tests they had taken in previous years. Instead of focusing on procedures and facts, it asked them to demonstrate their understanding of concepts (see Figure 4–4). The essays they wrote were as disappointing as the test results, so I created a structured set of directions for this essay (see Figure 4–5), and the results were much better. As the year progresses, and the students become more accustomed to writing essays, such detailed prompts are unnecessary, but it makes a big difference early in the year.

✔

Bean Probability Essay (4-blues 1-red)

What I think will happen is that there will be more mix's of red and blue then matches of blue and blue. The reason for that is that if you mix of shake up the beans and you take out three, there is a better chance of taking three blues instead of one red and two blues. Now I'm going to do it:

<u>Mix</u>   <u>Match</u>

卌   卌

What realy happened as you can see I got a tie. My group add up was 18 matches and 27 mix's including mine. our odds were: six matches and four mixs. So as you can see our   estimation came out wrong. Our picking was half and half. It was supposed to be two or a little more matches then mixes.

1° Math 卌

FIGURE 4–2

Dear 4th Grader,

I heard you wanted to know all about circles. I'm going to teach you everything they don't teach on "Sesame Street"! By now, I'm sure you know of a famous greek letter called PI (no, not cherry!). What! You don't? Well, PI is an _extremely_ famous irrational number (a number that can't be divided). It represents the ratio of a circle's circumference to it's diameter. (I'll get into those later.) It goes on continually. But all you need to memorize is 3.1416.

Remember those words circumfrence and diameter? A circumference is the line that bounds a circle. A diameter is a line segment that passes through the center of a circle and has both endpoints on the circle.

Here are two new words for your vocab.: chord and radius. A chord is a line segment with both endpoints on the circle. A radius is a line segment with one endpoint on the circle and the other endpoint at the center.

Now that you know everything I must bid you farewell!

What are you still reading for? Scat!

FIGURE 4–3

MATH 7π QUIZ #1   Name _____

                                        Period _____

I. SHOW THE ELEMENTS OF EACH OF THE FOLLOWING SETS:
1) the set of whole numbers:
2) the set of counting numbers:
3) the set of square numbers:
4) the set of triangular numbers:

II. EXPLAIN WHY YOU THINK EACH OF THE SETS OF NUMBERS IN PART I WAS GIVEN ITS NAME:

III. GIVE EXAMPLES OF EACH OF THE FOLLOWING:
5) A Venn diagram showing what kind of TV show people like (use at least three different types of shows)
6) A bar graph showing the time you spend on homework each day of the week

IV. CONSECUTIVE SUMS ACTIVITY
7) What patterns did your group find in the Consecutive Sums Activity?
8) Write these numbers as the sum of consecutive natural numbers in as many ways as possible: 17=   24=   25=
9) List the first 10 consecutive sums which are impossible.

V. EXPONENTS
10) Explain how exponents are related to multiplication. Show several examples.
11) Show the multiplication problem and the simplified answer to each of these exponential expressions:

$5^3=$ $2^9=$ $1^{15}=$ $256^0=$

VI. MEASUREMENT
12) Name something in this classroom which has a length of about one centimeter.
13) Name something which has the length of about one meter.
14) How many centimeters are in half a meter?
15) About how far (in centimeters) is the ceiling of this classroom from the floor?

VII. BOUNCE POD (explain your work completely)
16) If you were to use the same ball that was used by the girl in the POD, and you dropped it from a height of 256 feet, how high would it bounce after the sixth bounce?
17) If the ball from the POD bounced one inch after the tenth bounce, from what height was it originally dropped?

VIII. BONUS
Write 54 as the sum of consecutive natural numbers in at least two different ways.

FIGURE 4—4

QUIZ RESULTS ESSAY

Write a five-paragraph essay about the quiz you just took. Include your thoughts on each of the following:

1) **WHAT DID YOU DO TO PREPARE FOR THE QUIZ?**
   How much did you study? How did you study? Did you study with a partner or study group?

2) **HOW DID YOU FEEL BEFORE YOU TOOK THE QUIZ?**
   Were you nervous? Did the prospect of a test scare you? What were you most scared of? How did you think you would do on the quiz?

3) **WHAT DID YOU THINK WHEN YOU FIRST SAW THE QUIZ?**
   Did it look easy or hard? Did you see any questions that you knew for sure you'd get right? Did you see any questions that you didn't expect?

4) **HOW DID YOU DO ON THE QUIZ?**
   What score did you get? Do you think that this is a fair grade for you? Does the grade reflect how much you've learned about the material covered on the quiz?

5) **WHAT SHOULD YOU DO NEXT?**
   What could you have done to better prepare for this quiz? What do you plan to do to improve on future quizzes? What suggestions do you have for students who didn't do very well on the quiz?

FIGURE 4–5

Notebooks and Journals

My students are required to keep a detailed record of the activities we do in class. I tell them at the beginning of the year that they will be writing their own textbook for the class. Their math notebook is their own personal reference book, and they are allowed to use it throughout the course—on all classwork, homework, and tests. This is naturally a big incentive for them to take good notes. I give them some specific notebook guidelines (see Figure 4–6) and check the notebooks frequently during the first quarter of the year to make sure they're on the right track. In addition, we keep an "official class notebook" made up of copies of exemplary student-notebook pages. This official notebook is used as a reference against which all students can double-check their notes and is especially valuable for students who return to school after an absence.

I have used math journals in various forms over the years. Four years ago (the last year I taught in a completely tracked system), I taught a class of students in the bottom math level. These students had a very low self-concept, and one of my major goals was to improve their belief in their ability to do mathematics. One way I tried to do this was through a math journal. The journal was a spiral notebook (which they brought or I provided). The students were asked to include three things in each daily entry: what we did in class, what they thought of it, and what they learned from it (see Figure 4–7). I agreed to give them five minutes at the end of each class period in which to write their entries, a major concession on my part, since we always seemed to run out of time no matter what activity we were doing.

They soon got into the habit. In fact, five minutes before the end of the period, no matter what else we were doing, someone in the class would announce, "Journals!" and everyone would get out their journals and start writing. I collected the journals every Friday, read them and wrote back comments over the weekend, and returned them on Monday. I was struck by how eager they were to see what I had written back to them. They would spend the first few minutes of class on Monday reading my responses. At the beginning of the year, my responses were sometimes longer than their journal entries, but as we began to connect with each other through our writing and as they developed a greater trust in me and in their own mathematical abilities, their entries became longer and more informative.

MATH NOTEBOOK GUIDELINES

1) Use a notebook with pages that won't fall out. Write your name and class period on the outside cover.

2) Begin each day's work with a new side of the paper. Date the work.

3) Use part of the page for notetaking and part of notemaking. Your own comments are at least as important as the notes themselves.

4) Write neatly.

5) Use charts and diagrams as often as possible.

6) Highlight vocabulary words and key ideas.

7) Include a summary statement at the end of each day's lesson.

8) Keep your notes organized. Number the pages and create a table of contents or index.

FIGURE 4–6

MATH 8B JOURNAL

Your math journal is a record of your experiences and learning in this class. The purposes of the journal are: (1) to get you to think about your own learning and therefore come to a clearer understanding of the mathematics we are studying; and (2) to give me feedback on what you think of the various learning activities so that I may adjust the class to meet your needs.

Please write in your journal every day. I'll try to give you some time in class to do this, but you may have to do some writing outside of class on some days. Your journal is to be turned in by the end of the day each Friday. I will read it, make comments on it, and return it to you at the beginning of the period on Mondays.

Your journal must have <u>at least</u> the following three parts each day:

(1) WHAT WE DID
This section should include a detailed description of what we did in class that day. If there was more than one activity, describe each of them. Use complete sentences.

Example: *Today we did a group activity called pentominoes. We had to find all the possible arrangements of five squares. This is a sample:*

(2) WHAT YOU THOUGHT OF IT
This section is for you to tell me what you thought of the activity. Was it too easy? too hard? boring? interesting? too noisy? too quiet? Use complete sentences.

Example: *This activity was easy and fun. We had a chance to work together and we got all of the possible pentominoes. We should do more of these kinds of activities.*

(3) WHAT YOU LEARNED
In this section, you have to give some thought to what you learned from the activity. What did you learn about mathematics and about yourself? This is the most important part of the journal. Give it some serious thought. Use complete sentences.

Example: *I learned that there are __ pentominoes which is more than I thought there would be. I also learned that slides, flips, and turns create different-looking pentominoes.*

Your journal is an important part of this class. Be sure to write in it every day.

FIGURE 4–7

They opened up about more than just what we did, what they thought of it, and what they learned. Some students wrote more than a page every day, often sharing personal information not directly related to our math class. But in a real sense, everything they wrote was part of the class, because we were communicating and developing trust. The hour or two it took to read the journals and write comments back to the students was very important to that class, and I'm glad I did it. Obviously, this isn't something I could do in all my classes or even in one class every year, but in that special circumstance it was well worth the time commitment. Those journals that year changed me as a teacher. They gave me a real insight into the damage that tracking can do to students, and they made me want to try something different.

I currently use journals somewhat differently. I ask students to respond to certain journal questions as a way of getting feedback and sparking discussions about issues. The questions (see Figure 4–8) deal with topics related to our class activities or to the larger issues of math and learning.

Communicating About Mathematics

The problem-solving process described in Chapter 3 details the importance of having students learn to communicate mathematical concepts and ideas. It takes a little while for them to adjust to the scoring system, which deemphasizes the answer, but within a quarter or two, they are almost all experienced problem solvers and good mathematical writers. I am amazed at how quickly student writing improves when they are given good models and lots of practice.

Although very few of my present students speak a language other than English at home, I've had some experience teaching students with limited English proficiency (LEP), and I've worked with teachers at schools where primary languages other than English predominate. When the goal of math classes was the acquisition of computational skills, language proficiency was rarely an issue. However, changing our math curriculum to incorporate more language-based activities clearly creates problems for students with language deficiencies. We need to reexamine our traditional practice of mainstreaming LEP students in math classes, and we need to modify our expectations for some students until their ability to use the language improves. But we cannot assume that because certain students are not proficient in English, they are

QUICK-WRITE/JOURNAL QUESTIONS

- How was your first day of school?
- What is MATHEMATICS?
- What math did you use during the summer?
- What mathematics is there on your way to school?
- What does learning mean to you?
- How do you learn best?
- What did you learn this week?
- What does it mean to be smart?
- How do you rate yourself as a math student? Why?
- What challenges you the most in school?
- What do you enjoy the most about school?
- Describe a math teacher's job.
- What makes a good teacher?
- What is the best way to become an excellent student?
- If you could learn only one thing in math this year, what would you like it to be?
- What do you do really well in math?
- What do you like best about this class?
- What would you like to change about this class?
- How do you feel about using calculators in math class?
- What is your favorite number and why?
- What is your favorite math topic and why?
- What speaker would you like to invite to class and what two questions would you like to ask him/her?
- "Homework + Determination = Success" Do you agree or disagree? Why?
- Why is school important?
- What is your goal for this quarter in math?
- Helping other people is important because ...
- Sharing with other people is important because ...
- When I don't understand how to solve a problem, I ...
- Write at least three sentences to complete this statement: "When I work in a group, ..."
- How is this year's class different from last year's? How is it the same?
- Write a letter to an incoming seventh grader telling him/her what to expect next year in math.

Figure 4–8

therefore to be locked out of the learning opportunities given to other students.

As I've said, I believe that the *act* of writing is the key to understanding and learning. Students learn more and understand more deeply when they think about and write about their learning experiences. It makes little difference to individual students if they do that writing in their primary language rather than in English. It does, however, make a great deal of difference to the teacher who cannot read and understand the students' primary language. Assessment of student progress is almost impossible, and the ability of a teacher to comment on a student's work, provide encouragement and suggestions, is also lost. However, when we consider that there are three objectives for using student writing in mathematics—as a way to get students to reflect on their thinking, as a way to teach them to communicate about mathematics, and as a vehicle for assessment—achieving two of the three is far better than denying LEP students access to a rich math curriculum.

Sad Stories
Writing opens new doors of communication for students. It allows them to express themselves with creativity and humor. Sad stories are a perfect example. One year, I got tired of hearing the same old excuses for not completing homework: "My dog ate it." "It was in my pocket and it went through the wash." So I told students that in order to receive full credit for a late homework assignment, they would have to write a sad story about why they couldn't complete the assignment on time. If the story was sad enough, they'd be given full credit for the late assignment when they turned it in the next day.

I didn't realize how popular sad stories would become. I have a thick file of the stories students have submitted over the years. Some are three or four pages long and obviously took longer for the student to write than the original assignment would have taken. Some are tear-stained, some are full of violence, some are sarcastic, but all of them are excellent examples of students having fun with writing. I've had to put a restriction of one sad story per student per quarter because students like this creative outlet so much.

The sad stories in Figures 4–9 and 4–10, the first by a seventh grader, the second by an eighth grader, illustrate the differences between the two ages in the level of sophistication of their humor. The seventh

Dear Mr. Tsurada,

Please give me until Tuesday, January 29, 1991 to turn in last nights homework.

I haven't had a good week so far. On Monday, I was ran over by a semi driven by a man with a mowhawk and three teeth named Mad Dog. On Tuesday my uncle was viciously attacked by Mr. Mathiot while walking his dog. Yesterday my house burnt down—with my family in it. I was sent to an orphanage in east LA, from where I must walk to school here—in Palo Alto. This morning—after the toilet broke and I stubbed my toe on a street curb, getting the newspaper—I was attacked by a gang of dogs trained to take purses from old ladies. The dogs ran off with my backpack, which had my homework in it.

Painfully,

P.S. It pains me to write this to you because of a large gash left in my writing arm—left by the leader of the dog pack.

FIGURE 4–9

Sad Story 10/11

There I was, ready to turn in my great math homework for my wonderful math class and great teacher. I worked on it for four and one-half hours checking it ten times and making sure it was perfect <u>as ussual.</u> As I was searching for it in my very organized notebook, of course. I seemed not to have found it! I then realized that when I fell of my bike and skidded ten feet on my head when I was hurring to school because I knew a tardy would shater my life forever! After the accident a great big earthquake happened and swallomed me up! I grabed on to the pathway with one hand and homework paper in my other. So there I was. Dangaling, about to fall down and be swallowed by earth. I couldn't hold on much longer with one hand. I knew I would have to let go of whatever was in my other hand. I looked at the paper, and it was my math homework! I felt tears comeing down my cheek. I would have to miss a math homework! I was crushed. By now there were tens of people gathered around me yelling to let go of the paper. But I couldn't. Finally down to one finger I sliped luckily I grabed it again. But now...... with two hands! I pulled my self out destroyed! I couldn't go on. But i knew my perfect attendense record was at stake.

FIGURE 4-10

I got on my bike and went to school. But, (I can't believe it either) I forgot I lost the paper! It must have been the drama or the fall of my bike which gave me temperary ~~amnese~~ brain memory problam! Atleast I wasen't late to homeroon and got my memory back to tell you the story. I can truely say, I lived to tell about it!! (but lost my math paper). Now that my future is ruined, I hope you can count this paper for what I can barely bring myself to say, a very very sad story.

FIGURE 4–10 *(continued)*

grader's letter uses imaginative humor very creatively, while the eighth grader's letter uses sarcasm to poke fun at the whole idea of missing a homework assignment.

To reiterate what I stated at the beginning of the chapter, writing in mathematics (or in any other subject) accomplishes at least three objectives. It allows students to reflect on their own thinking and therefore gain insights into what they are learning. (A good example of this is the "What I Learned from Today's Activity" essays.) Writing also teaches students the value of communicating about mathematics (as they learn to do when they justify their thinking in POWs and other activities, for example). Finally, writing provides the teacher with a window into a student's thinking, thus creating an excellent means of assessing student learning. Never again will I teach mathematics without using writing, and I recommend incorporating some form of student writing into your teaching if you would like to begin to transform your teaching to reflect a more constructivist point of view. Like the use of POWs, writing is easy to add to any classroom structure, and it provides some real insights into what students are thinking and learning.

Assessment Alternatives 5

It is an unfortunate reality that assessment policies often drive curriculum practices. Although teachers may want to change how and what they teach in their classrooms, they are bound by their districts to administer tests that measure skills. Since constructivist teaching, which emphasizes thinking and communicating, is not the quickest way to help students acquire specific skills, and since all teachers feel a certain degree of pressure to have their students do well, teachers are caught in a dilemma.

External Assessment
Some teachers feel they would do their students a disservice by not preparing them for achievement tests and therefore either reduce or eliminate teaching practices that involve students' thinking about and learning concepts that are not easily tested. For others it's a question of job security; their evaluations are based in part on the achievement test results of their students. My advice to these teachers is to work hard at educating the decision makers in the district about the need to eliminate or change the tests. When there is enough demand for change, the publishers of the tests will change them. In the meantime, try to incorporate as many constructivist methods in your teaching as possible.

Teaching skills isn't a mortal sin. All students need to possess certain skills in order to "do" mathematics. The problem with many tests is the degree of emphasis they place on mathematical skills. We can no longer afford to spend up to 90 percent of our classroom time on pencil-and-paper computation, especially when the mode of instruction is primarily rote memorization of procedures.

If we approach skills as tools and embed them in mathematical investigations, students are much more likely to understand, personalize, and therefore remember the procedures we want them to know. Students who are working on an investigation involving circles with dimensions measured to the nearest sixteenth of an inch will want to know how to change those sixteenths to decimals in order to work with them more easily. This is the ideal time to introduce the concept of estimating and to do some work on converting fractions to decimals, because the need to learn these things comes from the students rather than from the teacher. The class, or a group of students in the class, might take some time out from their circle investigation to examine the fraction-decimal connection and then return to the circles after a few days.

You probably noticed that in the above, I didn't mention how the students would be performing the calculations. Students who are asked to convert sixteenths into decimal form should be using a calculator. They should be asked to estimate the size of the resulting decimal within a certain range and they should understand why fractions imply division, but it doesn't make sense to have students dividing whole numbers by sixteen using pencil and paper. I realize that some of the standardized tests require this skill of students, but I also feel that at some point we as teachers need to exercise our professional judgment and do what we think is right, in spite of the tests. I recommend emphasizing estimation and then allowing your students to use calculators to examine many different fraction-decimal combinations so that the students get a sense of the numbers. When they encounter the same type of question on a multiple-choice test, they will be able to use estimation to eliminate some of the distracters and then can make a reasonable guess. Students in classes that spent hours doing long-division exercises may well do no better on this question anyway.

The standard achievement assessments are forms of external summary assessment. That is, they are not directly connected to the instructional program, and they are given at the end of a certain period of time or after a certain amount of material has been covered. We can try to change the form that this assessment takes, but we cannot eliminate it completely; external assessment is a fact of life in education.

Classroom Assessment
The assessment over which we as teachers have greater control is, fortunately, also that which has the most meaning to us and to our students' learning. This is the day-to-day formative assessment we continually make about our students. We get to "know" our students through our interactions with them during class and even outside class, through the essays they write, the questions they ask, the comments they make. In short, we assess our students all the time, and we're good at it. Teachers don't realize how valid and important these continuous, cumulative judgments about students are. Yet we often grade tests or look at scores on external measures and say to ourselves, "Oh, I know Jeremy can do better than that" or "This isn't a good measure of Lindsay's understanding. She must have had a bad day." We need to give ourselves credit

for the informal assessments we make and, at the same time, build alternative forms of assessment into our programs to give us an even clearer picture of how our students are doing.

One of the easiest ways of building in assessment is through student writing. In fact, writing and verbalizing form the core of all forms of alternative assessment. As I discussed in Chapter 4, one of the purposes of student writing is to give teachers insights into student learning. This is what assessment is all about.

Having students write about their thinking and about their learning can provide the teacher with rare insight into the development of mathematical power. Since mathematical power is much more than knowing facts and possessing skills, traditional assessments measure only a small fraction of the spectrum of mathematical power. Writing, on the other hand, lets us into the process component of mathematics. It can answer questions like "How?" and "Why?" and can reveal student attitudes of enthusiasm, persistence, and curiosity.

The beauty of student writing as an assessment tool lies in its being directly linked to instruction. A writing assignment in which students summarize a concept helps them develop the idea and helps the teacher assess their understanding of the concept. In addition, writing is extremely easy to incorporate into any math program regardless of structure and format.

Open-ended questions are a product of the philosophy that students learn by constructing their own knowledge. If we want students to think about mathematics and express what they know and how the came to know it, then open-ended questions are a key form of assessment. An open-ended question gives students an opportunity to respond in a variety of correct and appropriate ways; there isn't only one right answer and the teacher isn't the only one who knows that answer. Nor should students be given open-ended questions only on external evaluations. Their daily experiences and assignments often should also take an open-ended form. The teacher might ask the students to formulate a hypothesis, explain a mathematical pattern, or make a generalization. This type of teaching works very well with cooperative groups. I often ask students to think about a particular idea and discuss it in their groups, their purpose being to develop a conjecture about it. Sometimes this idea is a pattern to examine and generalize from, sometimes it's an interesting numerical outcome to a problem, but it's always an idea worth thinking about, discussing, and exploring together. It's clear that traditional skill-based instruction doesn't fit this mode of instruction and assessment.

Other forms of assessment that don't match traditional practice include student presentations, discussions, and debates. All of these activities involve students thinking about and communicating mathematical ideas. Although this makes them very much like writing, they differ from writing in one important way: they allow the students who are verbal but who lack writing skills to show how much they know. Often students with learning disabilities that make writing difficult do very well in oral presentations and discussions. I try to allow my students to present ideas orally as often as possible.

Certainly my students present their thinking with every Problem of the Week they solve. And in most other lessons they also have an opportunity to show the rest of the class their thoughts on various ideas, problems, and questions. Discussions take place during any class activity. Sometimes these discussions are structured to include the whole class, but most of the time they take place within small groups. Even shy students find it easy to share ideas in this safe setting among a few of their classmates. I assess my students informally by listening to these discussions and being aware of the thinking and the contributions of individuals.

Many teachers, instead of listening to the important conversations of their students, take advantage of the fact that their students are happily engaged in doing mathematics to take care of some clerical work or to check homework. This wastes a golden opportunity. To listen to the conversations of students who are engaged in mathematical discovery and learning is to catch a glimpse of their thinking, to view firsthand the construction of mathematical knowledge. What could be more valuable or important to a teacher than this?

There are a variety of ways to record and quantify the observations of group work. Some teachers like to carry around a clipboard and make notes on individual student interactions, which they later discuss with the students. Others prefer to keep general notes on the class as a whole and report these comments back to the class at the conclusion of the period or activity. Still others keep no notes at all, preferring to form holistic impressions of how students are performing in groups. I tend to lean toward the second approach, but I don't always wait until the end of the activity or period to comment on how groups or individuals are doing. I'll frequently stop students in the middle of an activity to discuss the progress certain groups are making or to compliment certain groups or individuals for some outstanding contribution.

Any of these ways of informally assessing group work can be effective. Which is best for any individual teacher depends on the class and the teacher. The important component in all these ideas is the conscious assessment of group progress and the communication of that assessment to the students.

Debates are another excellent way to get students to think about and express themselves on issues related to mathematics. For example, I've used topics like whether students should be allowed to use calculators or the merits of the metric system as the basis for student debates. For this type of interaction, the "silent debate" works particularly well.

The format is simple. I pair students up and randomly assign the side of the question each is to take. For example, on tracking, one student is assigned to be in favor of math ability grouping, the other, opposed. These positions may be in direct opposition to their actual feelings about the issue, but they must suspend those beliefs for the debate.

Then the first student takes a sheet of paper and writes an opening statement for about two minutes while the other student considers possible arguments. After the allotted time, the first student passes the paper to the second student, who can either rebut the statement made by the first student or make an opposing opening statement.

This process is repeated as many times as the students seem capable of expressing their ideas at a high level. Throughout, nobody is allowed to talk; all debating takes place on paper. When the responses degenerate into name calling, it is time to move on to the next step. (With middle school students this typically happens after about three exchanges.)

The time allowed for each person to write depends on how much the students have to say about the subject. Two minutes is about right for the first statement or two, but thereafter, one minute is more than enough. After the silent part of the debate, I usually have students share their ideas in their small groups and then have each group share with the class.

There are a number of advantages to this type of debate. It is a way of getting *all* students to think about and express their ideas. In a regular debate format, the more verbal and aggressive students would tend to dominate, and shy students would be left out. The silent debate allows each student to have a voice. Forcing students to advocate a point of view that may be different from their own helps them see both sides of the issue and often diffuses some of the emotion that surfaces when students advocate something they feel strongly about. And, like any writing assignment, a silent debate forces students to organize their thinking and consider their audience, two extremely important considerations for all writers.

Portfolios

Three constructivist techniques have been critical to my excitement about and enjoyment of teaching: problem solving, writing, and portfolios. Having students solve real problems changed my thinking about how kids learn; having them write gave me insights into their thinking and helped them construct knowledge; and having them create portfolios allowed them to evaluate themselves and gave them a sense of pride in their learning.

Although portfolios are an excellent form of evaluation, I don't feel they are a good means of external assessment. That is, I don't think that a portfolio, by itself, is an effective way of evaluating a student's progress in mathematics. This may sound like blasphemy, since portfolios are currently a politically correct means of alternative evaluation. With few exceptions, I don't gain a great deal of information from student portfolios that I don't already know. I realize this is somewhat a function of the things I ask them to include, but I think it's very difficult for a portfolio to be used as a major source of information about student progress. The information gained from them needs to be used in conjunction with other information to form an overall picture of each student's progress.

Nevertheless, my experiences have shown me other important uses for portfolios. I've been using them for four years, and I've tried many different forms in that time. I started by having students review their work folders at the end of the year and reflect on that work, which consisted mostly of POWs, PODs, and a few essays.

This activity was so successful that the next year I decided to do it every quarter and to give my students a little more direction. Each succeeding quarter, I gave the students two weeks to choose a number of things to include in their portfolio. The work was done primarily outside of class and was graded on completeness. The final portfolio was a presentation of their entire year.

I've also used relatively open-ended portfolios. The assignment in Figure 5–1 is an example. Some of the material needed to be created by the student specifically for the portfolio, while other parts could be selected from previously completed assignments.

One of my most interesting experiments was a team portfolio for three subjects: English, math, and social studies. Two of the three teachers in our seventh grade team had used portfolios before and were planning to use them again. The third teacher wanted to try portfolios for the first time. We decided to have the students create a single portfolio including pieces of work from all three subjects. We discussed scoring rubrics and agreed that each of us would read thirty portfolios, evaluating all three subject areas. Reading the three-subject portfolios was especially enlightening, because seeing the students' best work in two other subjects gave me a more complete picture. The students reacted positively to the idea of doing three portfolios in one, and the quality and creativity of their work was amazing. I've found that the more opportunities students are given to express themselves creatively, the better I get to know them.

2ND QUARTER 1992-93 MATH PORTFOLIO

This portfolio is a collection of your work from the past quarter which represents you and your mathematical learning. Some of the work you have already completed, while other material will have to be created for this portfolio. For work which you select from your work folder, include a cover sheet that explains to the reader what your selection is about, what you thought of it, what you learned from it, and anything else you would like to include.

I. COVER LETTER: *(8 POINTS)* Give the reader an introduction to you and to your portfolio. Include <u>separate paragraphs</u> for each of the following:

1) Tell who you are and what you are like in your math class (how involved you get in the activities and discussions, how you work with others, how well you do on homework, tests, and problem solving), and any other information about yourself.

2) Describe how you have improved in math this quarter.

3) Describe your personal goals for the third quarter and tell how you plan to meet these goals.

4) Give the reader a summary of what he/she will be seeing in your portfolio.

II. PORTFOLIO CREATIONS *(12 POINTS)*

1) Write a summary of the key concepts we have covered during the second quarter. Limit yourself to 4 to 7 specific concepts. Explain each concept in detail, giving examples and illustrations.

2) Evaluate yourself for the quarter. Rate yourself in these categories: effort, learning, behavior, and how well you met the goals you set for yourself for the quarter.

3) Show one of the key concepts from the quarter in a creative form. You might make a drawing, write a poem or a story, make a poster, etc.

III. CHOICES (Be sure to include a cover sheet for each selection) *(9 POINTS)*

1) Choose a piece of work that shows **what you are good at** mathematically. Briefly explain what the assignment was and why you are especially proud of this work.

2) Choose a piece of work that shows **something you need to work on, improve at, or want to learn more about.** Explain what the assignment was and why you chose it.

3) Choose a piece of work that **you enjoyed.** Explain what the assignment was and why you enjoyed it.

IV. PRESENTATION *(6 POINTS)*

1) Assemble your work with a **cover sheet** which is creative and original, showing in graphic form (pictures, graphs, etc.) at least two of the key concepts you identified.

2) Include a **table of contents.**

3) Be sure that your work is **neat** and that it represents **the best that you can do.**

4) Review your portfolio with your parents and have them sign the **Parent Feedback Form.**

FIGURE 5-1

In my grading scheme, portfolios count for 15 percent of a student's overall grade and are evaluated once each grading period. The scoring system I use (see Figure 5–2) is based mostly on completion, so most students get good grades on their portfolios. I'm interested in having students reflect on their thinking and their work over the previous quarter, and the portfolio assignment serves this purpose. The relatively liberal scoring system is an incentive for the students to do the reflection and complete the assignment. Beyond completing the assignment and receiving a good grade, the students genuinely enjoy the reflective process and take pride in the progress they have made. Their introductory letters consistently reflect this pride of accomplishment.

I feel that the real value of portfolios, however, lies in the opportunity they provide for self-evaluation. Creating a portfolio requires students to reflect on past work and identify what they have learned. This process of metacognition is critical for the construction of knowledge, and it's an idea that we should share with our students. I talk about learning theory in my classes and discuss the value of practices like cooperative groups, writing, and metacognition.

Recently, I asked the students in my algebra class to create a different kind of portfolio. We'd been creating portfolios at the end of each three-to-four-week unit, and they were getting a little tired of them, so one day I announced that I had some good news and some bad news. The good news was that they wouldn't have to do a portfolio on the tiling rectangles unit, which dealt with factoring polynomials. (A cheer went up.) The bad news was that they would have to write a book instead. (This was greeted with a loud groan and an incredulous "What?!!")

I explained that their assignment was to write a book for next year's algebra class explaining how to factor any polynomial. I told them that if their books were good enough, we'd use them the following year and skip the tiling rectangles unit. I also asked them to make sure that their books were interesting, unlike the typical math textbook. The interest generated by the opportunity to be creative inspired some excited conversations as they brainstormed ideas for their factoring "books." Later in the period, however, one of the students exclaimed, "Oh, I get it! It's metacognition again . . . this is just a portfolio in disguise!"

The books, by the way, were outstanding. For example, "How an Ant Would Factor Quadratics" explored factoring as a series of different tunnels, with each branch leading to a different type of quadratic expression to be factored. "Voudoria and the Secret Magic of Factoring Quadratics," a thirty-two page story narrated by Igor the Minstrel, was set in the least advanced civilization on the planet, the Land of Mathematical Stupidity.

SECOND QUARTER MATH PORTFOLIO
ASSESSMENT FORM

Name _____

	POSSIBLE	YOUR SCORE
I. COVER LETTER		
1) Who you are and what you are like	3	_____
2) How you improved in math	2	_____
3) Personal goals and planning	2	_____
4) Summary for reader	1	_____
II. PORTFOLIO CREATIONS		
1) Key concepts, examples, illustrations	4	_____
2) Self-evaluation	4	_____
3) Illustrated key concepts	4	_____
III. CHOICES		
1) What you are good at	3	_____
2) Something to work on	3	_____
3) Something you enjoyed	3	_____
IV. PRESENTATION		
1) Cover sheet	1	_____
2) Table of contents	2	_____
3) Neatness and effort	2	_____
4) Parent feedback form`	1	_____
TOTAL	**35**	_____

FIGURE 5–2

Another student, claiming to be the author of the children's classic "Green X and Ham," wrote "Alice in Factorland," a children's book complete with illustrations. The teacher of the other algebra class at our school chose not to have his students write factoring books, so he gave his class the books my students had written and asked them to write book reviews. These thoughtful reviews were shared with my students, who were very anxious to see what other people thought of their creations.

The amazing creativity of these students opened new doors for me in my thinking about metacognition. I was able to break out of the standard format for portfolios I had been using and explore ways of allowing students to reflect and be creative at the same time. The next seventh-grade portfolio I assigned (see Figure 5–3) had many more opportunities for students to express themselves creatively about what they had learned. One part of the assignment, for example, asked them to write a short story or poem to illustrate the fact that geometry is all around us. They were also invited to write a newspaper article, draw a cartoon, or create an advertisement to illustrate a key idea we had studied.

The final portfolio assignment for this class was a relatively short one. It was called "The π Letters" and asked the students to write four letters: to the reader, introducing the portfolio and reviewing the year; to their sixth-grade teacher, sharing their seventh-grade math experiences; to Bobo, an incoming seventh grader, giving advice about succeeding in Math 7π; and to their eighth-grade teacher, introducing themselves and telling how they learn best in math. The assignment turned out to be a very good one. The students were very thoughtful in their writing and liked the assignment. Many of them commented on how this portfolio was a good way of looking back over the year. The portfolios were taken apart after scoring, and the letters were given to the sixth-grade teachers, the new seventh-grade students, and the eighth-grade teachers. All the recipients appreciated the information.

Portfolios are also an excellent means of communicating student progress to parents. I ask my students to show their portfolios to their parents before turning them in, and I invite parent comments on a parent feedback form (see Figure 5–4). Almost without exception, parents are very pleased with the quality and the depth of the work in the portfolios. They gain new insights into the math program as well as learn more about their children and the work they are capable of doing.

One thing I would like to do in conjunction with portfolios is to schedule student interviews. I'd like to sit down with students one-on-one and have them present their portfolios and projects to me. I'd like to be able to ask them about what they learned from specific learning

GEOMETRY PORTFOLIO
APRIL

This quarter's portfolio will focus on a single area of mathematics, geometry. Like the other portfolios you have done it will be a collection of your work which represents you and your mathematical learning.

I. COVER LETTER: Give the reader an introduction to your portfolio. Include separate paragraphs for each of the following: **(2 points for each paragraph)**

1) Give an overview of the portfolio; let the reader know what he/she will be seeing and what you thought about doing the portfolio. Add any additional information about yourself.

2) Review the goals you set for yourself for the third quarter and tell how well you achieved them.

3) Set goals for yourself for the fourth quarter and tell how you plan to meet them.

II. CREATIONS: These entries are original work to be created for this portfolio.

1) Draw, cut out of construction paper, or find a picture of each of the following polygons. (Some pictures may illustrate more than one polygon.) Be sure to label each picture: **(2 points each)**

a) scalene triangle	b) isosceles triangle	c) equilateral triangle
d) right triangle	e) parallelogram	f) rhombus
g) trapezoid	h) hexagon	i) octagon

2) Draw or find a picture of each of the following three-dimensional objects. Be sure to label each picture. **(2 points each)**

    a) cube   b) triangular prism   c) rectangular prism   d) sphere

3) Write a short story or poem to illustrate the fact that geometry is all over the place. Title the story or poem and include an illustration. **(8 points)**

4) Write an article, draw a cartoon, or write/draw an ad that illustrates one of the key ideas of geometry that we have studied. **(8 points)**

III. CHOICES: Include a single page cover sheet for each selection. On the cover sheet, explain to the reader what the selection is about, what you thought of it, what you learned from it, and any other information you would like to add. **(3 points each)**

1) Choose a piece of work that illustrates **something you enjoyed** during the quarter while learning about geometry.

2) Choose a piece of work that shows **something you learned** about geomtery during the quarter.

IV. PRESENTATION: **(2 points each)**

1) Create a cover which illustrates several of the key concepts of geometry in a creative way.

2) Be sure that your work is **neat** (use a ruler for all drawings, etc.) and represents **your best work.**

3) Review your portfolio with your parents and have them sign the **Parent Feedback Form.**

FIGURE 5–3

PARENT FEEDBACK FORM

Dear Parents,

This portfolio is one representation your child's mathematical learning during the second quarter in Math 7π. As you can see, it contains some work which was already completed as well as some newly-created material of a reflective nature. I feel that this opportunity for students to show their best work and to think about their learning is valuable in terms of assessment and instruction.

I would appreciate your taking the time to review the portfolio **with** your child. Please sign this form and include any comments about the portfolio, your child, or the class in general. Thank you for your interest in your child's educational progress.

Sincerely,

Gary Tsuruda

Comments: _____

_____
_____
_____
_____
_____
_____
_____
_____
_____
_____
_____
_____
_____

Parent signature _____

FIGURE 5–4

activities and to find out what areas they would like to explore further. This might be one of the best ways of assessing student progress, but it requires a significant amount of time. To date, I haven't been able to find a way to make this happen, but I am committed to making it happen someday soon.

We are very fortunate to be in the field of math education at this time. It's a period of tremendous growth and change, and the excitement is contagious. We're also fortunate that mathematics assessment is changing almost as rapidly as are curriculum and instruction. This has not always been the case; traditionally, modifications in assessment have lagged far behind curriculum changes, creating a difficult situation for teachers who wanted to keep up with the latest developments in curriculum but were worried that their students would do poorly on traditional assessments. To be sure, this is still true to some extent, but major changes in standardized tests are on the way. Students in California, for example, will be given open-ended questions and will be allowed adequate time to complete their answers as part of the new statewide California Learning Assessment System (CLAS). They'll even be allowed to use calculators and manipulative materials as part of the assessment.

The classroom assessments used by individual teachers are also changing to match the new approach to teaching and learning. Open-ended questions and writing are becoming more common on teacher-made tests, and grading schemes are placing more emphasis on complete student work than on tests of low-level skills and definitions. For example, in my classes of ten years ago, tests counted for as much as 75 percent of a student's overall grade, with homework making up the remaining 25 percent. My current plan includes five different categories, including homework, problem solving (PODs and POWs), tests, projects, and portfolios. The tests count for only 20 percent of a student's overall grade, and at least half of the tests involve open-ended questions.

There is still a great deal to be learned about how students learn best and how we can best assess the progress they are making. As is true for most of the other changes I've described, teachers have a great deal of control over the degree and the pace of the move away from traditional assessments. It's not something that will be successful if forced; it works best when the teacher is comfortable with and voluntarily initiates the change. We do, however, need to continue to move forward and challenge ourselves for the benefit of the students. As Will Rogers said, "Even if you're on the right track, you'll get run over if you just sit there."

Grouping Practices

6

Instructional organization can take many forms. This chapter examines institutional organization—tracking—as well as classroom organization. Although they come under the same broad heading, they are very different situations. Both involve the grouping of students and both are at the forefront of reform in math instruction, but their similarities end there. Using cooperative groups in a *classroom* can be a successful teaching technique regardless of the *school's* grouping practice. And although it's difficult for me to imagine untracked mathematics classes that don't make use of cooperative groups, some don't.

Tracking

For most of my career, I have taught math classes in which the students were grouped by level of achievement. Some people refer to this as ability grouping, but this is a misnomer. Some students may have had the ability to do better than they did, but they were placed in groups according to how well they could perform certain tasks, mostly computational skills. Until fairly recently, I firmly believed, as did most math teachers, that this was the best way to teach mathematics. I considered math to be a linear, sequential, hierarchical subject, one that had to be learned in a certain order. Therefore, it made sense that students who were achieving at about the same level on this linear scale be placed in math classes together. It seemed that mixing students in classes would only create a less efficient system. The lower-level students would slow down the progress of the higher-level students and wouldn't be able to get the necessary individual instruction in order to "catch up."

I was well aware of the concerns about the self-esteem of low-achieving students in a tracked system. My solution was to create a low-level class that covered a practical curriculum, used calculators every day, and incorporated a great deal of student involvement. For several years, I taught a class called Special Math for low-achieving students. We didn't use a textbook; most of the work dealt with real-life math skills such as consumer math, so we used quite a few manipulatives. We played math games to illustrate ideas and used calculators freely, a very novel approach in those days. Developing self-esteem was a high priority. I enjoyed teaching Special Math, and I learned quite a bit about teaching and about curriculum by creating that program.

The students liked the class as well. They enjoyed the curriculum because it was fun and it made sense to them, and they did well, at least for the time they were in the class. When they moved on, however, they were forced back into the realities of the school system. They were placed in low-level remedial math classes in high school, and many of them simply didn't make it. For years I blamed their failure on the system. I felt that the Special Math curriculum had worked for these students and that they could have been successful if a similar modification had been made for them in high school.

Several years later, I ran into one of my former Special Math students. We reminisced about the class and he told me how much he had enjoyed it. But then he told me something else that opened my eyes to what the class had failed to do. He said that even though he liked the class and learned a lot, he was always aware that it was "a dummy class" and no matter what, he still felt dumb when he left. In other words, even though I had tried to provide the best instruction possible with an inviting and practical curriculum, I couldn't remove the social stigma imposed by the school's grouping practice.

When we create achievement groups, we need to be aware that the simple *existence* of different levels can create devastating long-term self-image problems for students at the bottom end of the scale, no matter what we do with that bottom end class. And the longer students are in "ability" groups, the greater the differences in their achievement levels tend to become, so when we create tracks in our math program, we build boxes for students at the low end from which they might never escape.

The 1992 California State *Mathematics Framework* calls for heterogeneous grouping of students in classes through eighth grade. Throughout the discussions that led to the *Framework*, I was skeptical about this position. I knew that "ability" grouping was not good for low-achieving students, but I wasn't so sure about the students at the upper end of the scale. Wouldn't heterogeneous grouping hold them back? I understood the arguments about students helping and learning from one another, but I maintained that when the differences in achievement level were too high, it wouldn't work. Besides, I argued, there were very few exemplars of this type of instruction and therefore no proof that it *could* work.

I now believe that I was both right and wrong in my beliefs about "ability" grouping. I think I was right about the lack of guarantees and the limited number of models for the program we were advocating, but I have a different view about whether or not heterogeneous grouping can work. Since I've been working with classes that are relatively heterogeneous (all but the "gifted" seventh graders), I've found instructional materials that can meet the needs of this wide range. I've seen students who would have been placed in a low-level class produce outstanding work and show insight that I would never have expected. The research evidence is convincing as well. There is no strong evidence that "ability" grouping produces any educational benefits for students at any level, and there is a great deal of evidence that it does educational and social damage to students at the low end of the scale.

In spite of the overwhelming research base in favor of eliminating "ability" grouping, it persists as a practice in many math classes. There are a number of reasons for this, including the failure to understand constructivism, a curriculum that is heavily oriented toward computational skills, the shortage of materials suitable for heterogeneous instruction, the fear of the unknown, and simple inertia ("we've always done it like this").

Teachers who don't believe that students learn by constructing their own knowledge, who still think that teaching is telling, have a hard time believing that untracking will work, because they know how difficult it is to teach anything to kids in the low tracks. They think that telling works because the kids in the higher levels seem to do well when we lecture to them and give them procedures for solving problems. They miss the fact that *all* learning is constructed by students. The students in the top tracks are able to take our lectures and our procedures, synthesize the ideas, and construct their own knowledge. We tend to categorize and separate out those students who can't synthesize as quickly, calling them "slow learners," when in fact they may be able to do just as well when the material from which they are asked to construct knowledge is presented in a richer, more stimulating mathematical setting.

If a curriculum emphasizes the acquisition of pencil-and-paper computational skills, then it tends to be hierarchical in nature. In fact, it is this very emphasis on the mastery of skills that leads teachers to think of all mathematics as sequential and hierarchical. In reality, mathematics is much broader and more interesting than the small piece of it we have chosen to show to students. A skill-oriented curriculum punishes students with the drill and memorization of number manipulation and refuses to acknowledge the fact that mathematics is the study of patterns and that the true beauty and power of mathematics lies in that study. Is it any wonder that students' attitudes toward mathematics diminish as they proceed through the educational system? The key to change here is the acceptance of a broader view of what mathematics is and what parts of mathematics are important for students to know.

The limited availability of materials that can be used with untracked classes is a problem. The materials are out there, but at present they are not easily accessible. Teachers trying to work with heterogeneous classes are putting together their own curricula, drawing on excellent materials from a variety of sources. This is a very time-consuming and difficult task, but many dedicated teachers are doing it every day. What is needed for significant change to occur is large-scale curriculum development and organization. Publishers need to be assured that a major segment of the mathematics teaching profession is ready for this material. Until they see a significant market for the product, they aren't going to invest millions of dollars to produce it.

One of the strongest inhibitors to change is inertia. It's much easier to continue to do things the same old way than it is to make changes, especially when those changes involve more work. This is not to say that teachers are lazy or that they don't care about kids. Absolutely not! Teachers are among the hardest-working professionals in the country and the vast majority of them care very much about their students. This is precisely why inertia is such a strong factor in educational change. Teachers who have worked hard to develop a certain curriculum and who feel they are doing the best they can for their students cannot be faulted or criticized for not jumping on the latest educational bandwagon without first asking a few questions. Change is difficult for many of us to accept, perhaps even more so for those who have worked the hardest to make things work for their students.

Making the transition to alternative grouping practices involves addressing each of the concerns just described. Teachers who are interested in examining their programs and perhaps moving away from tracking should first realize that untracking is not a goal in itself. Rather, it is a means to an end, a very important tool for helping us attain a larger goal—better education for all students. Incorporating a more constructivist philosophy into their teaching will help teachers see that a wide range of students *can* learn together in the same classroom and can benefit from one another. And when the focus of the curriculum shifts away from computational skills, the need to group students becomes less apparent. We all need to work together to learn as much as we can about this new approach by trying out different parts of it with our students and keeping an open mind. When parts of the approach seem comfortable, we should let the producers of mathematics instructional materials know that we would like to see things that will help make our jobs easier.

As a teacher who has tried many different approaches with many different types and levels of students, I have come a long way in these past few years. I've gone from being a skeptic and a detractor of heterogeneous grouping to a supporter. I'm still skeptical about some aspects of total untracking, but I'm trying to work through these concerns. I am convinced that what I'm doing with my students now is much better than what I used to do with Special Math, and I hope to work with completely heterogeneous classes in the near future. It's a major challenge facing us as math teachers, and I'm confident that we'll be able to make it work for our students.

Cooperative Groups

Having students work in cooperative groups isn't new, nor is the practice the exclusive province of math teachers. Cooperative groups are an excellent way to meet the needs of a group of students with different achievement levels. By the same token, it is certainly possible to use cooperative groups in tracked classes as well. I started using groups in my classes ten years before I began to deal with more heterogeneous classes.

When I first began using groups, I used them as part of a management system. Students worked together, discussed ideas, and sometimes competed against other groups in group challenges. Over the years, I've tried groups of four and groups of six; I've carefully selected the groups myself, allowed the students to self-select their groups, and selected the groups randomly; and I've kept the same groups for a week, two weeks, three weeks, or a month. The system I've settled on and have been happy with for the past four years uses randomly selected groups of four every week.

I pick groups of four because this number seems to work best for most of the activities I use. When an activity calls for pairs, the group of four easily becomes two pairs. For most discussions, four seems the optimum number for both diversity and manageability. When the number of students in a class is not a multiple of four, I create groups of three with the "extra" students rather than groups of five or six. Larger groups tend to evolve into two smaller groups anyway, so I have found it easier to simply start out small.

I assign students to groups through a card system. My classroom desks are always arranged in groups of four, and each group of desks is labeled with the name of a branch of mathematics: calculus, algebra, arithmetic, trigonometry, etc. I have a set of cards labeled with the names of each group (four cards with each group name), which are shuffled and dealt out to the students at the beginning of the period every Monday. When everyone has a card, I say, "On your marks, get set, go!" and start the stopwatch. Each student must move to the appropriate group and sit down without talking or slamming books. When the last person sits down, I stop the stopwatch and announce the time. I've used this method with my classes every week for the past four years, and they haven't tired of it. They still try to get low times, even though there is no tangible reward. (So far, the unofficial "world record" for changing seats is 4.65 seconds, set by a class of twenty-eight seventh graders on March 8, 1993.)

The advantages to this system involve logistics and socialization. Logistically, the system is easy to operate. The entire process takes only a few minutes, and I ask student assistants to complete the formal seating charts each week. Changing groups weekly makes it easier to appease students who complain about the people in their group: I just tell them that in a few more days, they'll get a new group, but in the meantime, they must make the best of it.

This brings up the socialization aspect of frequent random grouping. I want students to learn how to work well with a variety of other students, some whom they like, others whom they dislike. I also want them to experience the classroom from a variety of perspectives. Some students, when offered a choice, will always sit at the front of the room seeking the attention of the teacher and/or their peers. Others will always sit at the back of the room. When I was in school, I always tried to "hide" in the back because of my shyness. I think it's better for students to experience the class from a variety of groups within the classroom. Using groups helps students appreciate the talents and abilities of their classmates. As we study various branches of mathematics, different students show that they are "smart" in certain areas.

Some educators advocate assigning roles to students in their groups. They feel that students are empowered by being assigned roles like facilitator, materials manager, recorder, reporter, and harmonizer. I have resisted making these assignments even though I can see that doing so might raise the status of certain students who might not otherwise take on some of the roles seen as more important. One reason I haven't used this system is because I remember what it was like to be an extremely shy student. I couldn't possibly have been a group facilitator or a reporter. I might have gone through the motions in order to avoid the disapproval of my teacher, but I would have hated every minute of it, just as I hated making oral reports. Colleagues have told me that maybe I would have been able to overcome my shyness by being forced into these roles, but that certainly wasn't the case with the oral reports I was forced to give and spelling bees in which I was forced to participate.

My other concern with assigning group roles is the exclusionary nature of the roles. If one person is assigned to be the facilitator or the harmonizer, then it seems as if the rest of the group is excused from this responsibility. This works well for roles such as materials manager or recorder, which entail functions more effectively carried out by only one person, but I try to encourage *all* students to facilitate their group's ability to work together—to get everyone to participate and to help resolve conflicts. Assigning only one person to this task undermines the philosophy that every member of the group is responsible for making the group work. I make this point early in the year, and I reinforce it as often as possible thereafter. When a group member sees the group beginning to lose its focus or stray off-task, I want that person to feel responsible for helping to get the group back on target. I don't want three people to sit back and watch a group fall apart simply because somebody else was assigned the role of facilitator.

On the other hand, I know some outstanding teachers who use group roles and are very happy with the results. I'm not completely convinced, but I respect the judgment of my colleagues, so I'm going to try a modified form of group roles in an attempt to make it work for me. I still won't assign a facilitator or a reporter, but I may use other roles, perhaps timekeeper or organizer or teacher liaison.

Group activities are meant to encourage discussion and participation among the group members as they investigate a mathematical idea. It's best at first to keep the mathematics relatively easy (but not so easy that the students are not challenged or engaged). The goal for the first part of the year is to learn the culture of group work. The students need to learn appropriate group behavior, the process of asking for help (for example, I will only answer a question when all students in the group have the same question and raise their hand), and the reasons for working in groups. Students learn this culture through their experiences in groups and the discussions about their work in groups. I also ask my students to evaluate their group work and find ways to improve (see the Group Activity Evaluation in Figure 6–1). Occasionally I may ask them to write essays about group work. I once asked the students to write about the meaning of the word *cooperation*. Another assignment was to write about what it means to "help" another student. The essay included as Figure 6–2 was one student's very creative response.

Perhaps the most critical aspect of group work with regard to learning is the forum it creates for discussion. When students are placed in situations in which they must verbalize their thoughts and ideas, their thinking, of necessity, becomes clearer. I see students who struggle to communicate about mathematics at the beginning of the year make tremendous growth in their writing and verbal skills, and I'm convinced that the process of having to explain and defend their ideas helps them clarify mathematical concepts.

Cooperative groups are an integral part of the structure of my classroom. Students are involved in group activities or discussions almost every day. This doesn't mean we never have whole-class discussions or presentations. We start each day with some form of whole-class presentation, and most small-group discussions lead to whole-class follow-ups. But the predominant form of mathematical exploration is in groups of four. I am so comfortable with this format now that I can't imagine not using it.

For those who are interested in using cooperative groups for the first time, I suggest starting slowly, perhaps using groups for a single unit and then assessing how it went. It's important to keep in mind that getting students to work effectively in groups takes time: don't be discouraged if things don't go smoothly from the first day. Remember that the initial phase of group work is getting students to buy into the culture of working together.

Once that is accomplished, cooperative groups can become a powerful learning experience for students and for teachers. Groups give students an opportunity to take more responsibility for their own

GROUP ACTIVITY EVALUATION

Date_____   GROUP_____   Name_____

PLEASE RATE YOUR PARTICIPATION IN THE GROUP ACTIVITY BY RESPONDING TO
EACH OF THE FOLLOWING ITEMS AS CAREFULLY AND HONESTLY AS YOU CAN.

NOT AT ALL   SOMETIMES   OFTEN

_____   _____   _____   (1) I helped organize our group.

_____   _____   _____   (2) I listened to others' ideas.

_____   _____   _____   (3) I offered suggestions.

_____   _____   _____   (4) I explained things to others in my
                                              group.

_____   _____   _____   (5) I stayed on task.

_____   _____   _____   (6) I asked my group for help.

_____   _____   _____   (7) I encouraged and complimented
                                              others.

_____   _____   _____   (8) I shared materials.

_____   _____   _____   (9) I enjoyed the activity.

_____   _____   _____   (10) I enjoyed the people in my group.

Some ways our group worked well were_____

_____

_____

Our group could have worked better by_____

_____

_____

This activity could have been improved by_____

_____

_____

FIGURE 6–1

```
                               math
                               period 6    10/10


              WHAT DOES IT MEAN TO COOPERATE?

     "What are you doing you dummy?  Thats wrong !" or
     "No, we are going to do it my way!"
      These are words that come out of people's mouths when they are not
   being patient, and are not trying to make the group effort really shine
   through.  Sometimes when I am in a group I feel I would rather be with my
   friends but I make an effort to really try to bring everybody together as a
   group.
      Today all we accomplished in my group( which I think is statistics ? )
   was to barely start working on connecting the blocks.  I really wish we
   could have finished because it was going really well !  Not one person
   spoke out of turn and no one said anything negative.  I thought that we
   were really doing a good job on our group effort and I hope we do another
   group project soon so I can compare.
```

FIGURE 6–2

learning. When a group is given a task to accomplish, certain roles need to be filled, and it becomes obvious to students that they may have to fill several of those roles during the course of the year, depending on the other students in their groups. By sitting in on group discussions, teachers are able to get a very good picture of the understandings and misunderstandings of the group. Moving from group to group, we can assess the relative strengths of individuals, the areas that need more reinforcement, and the overall level of understanding of the class.

        I pick up some of this information by asking questions directly, but I get most of it by simply listening to the dialogue *among* students. The window into the thinking of students this provides is enlightening, and I'm convinced that cooperative groups provide an organizational structure that supports the goal of having students construct their own knowledge.

Putting It Together 7

The differences between my teaching now and my teaching of ten years ago are unmistakable. Everything from the way my classroom looks to the way I deal with students is different. My classroom is much more lively now than it used to be; there is much more evidence that it's the students' room rather than mine. I still have posters on the wall and signs that I've made, but most of the wall space is taken up with student work, student pictures, student projects. By having students write first-impressions essays at the beginning of the school year, I have learned that the room environment is important to them. They like a colorful, neat, student-centered room, and they feel comfortable when they are surrounded by evidence of their own learning.

The number and type of group activities I now use have changed significantly over the years. I now ask students to discuss topics and share ideas much more than I used to. When I first started using groups, the amount of time the students spent in actual collaboration on problems or projects was limited: I might spend only part of a class period every other day on such activities. Now I try to have students work in their groups for the majority of the period almost every day. They frequently consult one another in order to solve problems, examine issues, develop theories.

I've always felt that my classes were well organized and that my students had a clear idea of what was expected of them. In the past those expectations dealt with rules for behavior, usually stated in terms of what *not* to do. My classes are still, in my opinion, well organized, and my students still have a clear idea of my expectations, but the tone is much more positive. A poster at the front of the room displays the class rules: Rule #1: Respect everyone's right to learn. Rule #2: See Rule #1. We discuss the reasons for what we do, and the students accept responsibility for learning. They take a more active role in the classroom than I allowed before. Students take roll, prepare materials for absent students, distribute and collect homework, control the classroom environment, and greet visitors. When students take on these responsibilities, they begin to take ownership of the classroom and their own learning. It brings us one step closer to the ideal situation in which all students understand and accept that we're here for a common purpose and that we are all responsible for helping to achieve that purpose.

Ten years ago, I spent most of the period presenting information to my classes. I spent hours preparing elaborate visuals and models in order to make my presentations more effective. The students were pretty much passive receptacles for the presentations I made, and some were much more passive than others. This model brings to mind the joke about an alien's conclusion about our school system: "School is a place where young people go to watch old people work." I work even harder now than I did ten years ago, but the work is of a different type. Most of my time now is spent planning and preparing for class. My class time with the students is more fun than work. I get to interact with them as they work on problems and discover new ideas. I still spend some of my time managing the classroom, but most of my day involves direct contact with individuals and small groups of students.

The work my students used to do was predominantly skill-based. The classwork and homework was usually a series of practice exercises. I used games and other activities to motivate the students and help them learn the skills more easily. Problem solving was an extra-credit activity, and writing was something done in the English class next door. Now my students work on activities and projects in their groups, they write about mathematics in some form every day, and they solve big, nonroutine problems almost every week.

I used to evaluate student progress primarily through test scores. Now I use a number of different methods of assessment, and testing accounts for a relatively small part of a student's overall grade. The self-assessment activities associated with writing activities and portfolios are a major part of my program.

As you can see, the differences are huge. None of these changes took place overnight. Some of them were hard to make, most involved some degree of risk because the approach I was changing from was perceived as very successful, and all of them are only benchmarks. In no way do I feel that I have "found the answer" to the question of the best way to teach. I'm learning more each day about better ways to teach, but there is no final "right answer." As in problem solving, in the search for the best way to teach, the *process* of finding a solution is more important than the answer.

Curriculum

Middle school mathematics is often described as nothing more than a rehash of the concepts and skills students have learned in elementary school. Studies of new content by grade level in textbook series bear this out to some degree: relatively few new concepts are introduced in grades six through eight. Some argue that this is necessary because middle school students are undergoing so many physical and social changes (as if their brains can't handle anything difficult because they are adolescents). I have not found this to be at all the case. Although the process of changing from a child to an adult seems to accelerate during the middle school years, these students are fully capable of accepting and meeting major intellectual challenges. In fact, middle school mathematics is seen by many math educators as key to the reform movement's success.

Many teachers let the textbook they use determine curriculum content. The table of contents and the scope and sequence charts lay out the concepts to be covered and the order in which they should be taught. Other teachers use their school or district guidelines to determine what should be taught, supplementing the textbook when necessary. For others, state frameworks or the NCTM *Standards* serve as guidelines as they plan their curriculum with or without a textbook. In each of these cases, the teacher has a great deal of control over what is taught and how it is taught. It may not seem like control when a department head or a district administrator specifies content to a teacher, but it is: teachers have great freedom of choice, even within relatively strict guidelines. Teachers determine the topics they want to emphasize and the order in which those topics are covered. Teachers also control, for the most part, their methods of instruction. My point is this: we teachers have a major responsibility to determine and implement our own curriculum. We cannot abdicate this responsibility to those who don't understand our students or share our vision for how students learn. Of course we need to make changes within the system, but we can't let the system keep us from doing what we know is right. It's too easy to make excuses for not trying new ideas at the expense of our principles and our students.

Getting Started

I realize that the ideas presented here may seem a bit overwhelming to those just beginning to think about modifying their approach to teaching mathematics. Keep in mind that the majority of the changes in my teaching took place over a period of approximately two years, and many of the ideas I've described in this book have taken a number of years to develop.

My own transition started with problem solving through POWs and cooperative grouping of students. When I gained new insight and confidence about the approach, I began to incorporate new ideas like writing and portfolios. Underlying these later changes was my understanding that students don't learn by being told but by experiencing mathematics and constructing their own knowledge. This understanding made it possible for me to refine the practices I had been using and to add new approaches with confidence.

If I were starting over again today, I would start by learning as much as I could about the latest views on how students learn. I feel strongly that this new approach is the key to the entire reform movement. I'd discuss these ideas with my colleagues, and I'd observe teachers who put the theory into practice. But mostly, I'd try it out in my own classroom. I'd use some lessons that embrace this philosophy and I'd honestly critique them and modify them to fit my style. I feel that to truly understand the principles of this new approach, one needs to experience them with students. I'm learning more about how students learn every day as I try new approaches to traditional concepts.

My advice to teachers who are beginning to incorporate new approaches into their teaching is to start slow. Don't try to do too much too soon. As exciting as these ideas are, they are somewhat self-limiting, and the limits are not determined by commitment but by time and energy. Don't attempt to do so much that you burn yourself out in a year or two. Be patient and try those ideas that feel right to you and are manageable. Be constantly aware of the difference between form and spirit; make sure that the ideas you are using are consistent with your philosophy, and don't be pressured into trying things because they "look right."

A relatively easy beginning may be to incorporate writing into the math curriculum. It's an easy first step because it fits well into any structure and can be done effectively on a very small scale. Cooperative groups are another good area in which to begin to make changes. Start by using groups for one or two activities or projects per quarter.

The next step I would suggest is to use Problems of the Day and Problems of the Week. I recommend starting with a few PODs early in the year and then trying three or four good POWs during the rest of the year.

Portfolios may seem like a lot of work, but they really aren't. I highly recommend trying them as an outstanding self-assessment tool for students. But again, start small; modify and add ideas as you and the students become more familiar with this new form of assessment.

If possible find a partner, a fellow teacher who is trying to incorporate some of these ideas into the classroom or who, like you, is willing to try out new approaches. Talking about new ideas, sharing successes and failures, and collaborating on new approaches are an important part of the process of change, and, believe me, they make the process much easier. I couldn't have made even half of the changes I've made without the support and encouragement of colleagues.

This is an exciting time to be a mathematics teacher. Change is all around us. Teachers are excited and involved in their profession as never before. But it's also a very difficult time. Many of our previous beliefs about teaching, about learning, about mathematics itself, are being challenged. And change itself is very threatening. We need to take the time to consider the new ideas and use the ones that make sense to us, and we need to work together to make the transition as smooth as possible. We need to talk to one another, to share ideas and points of view in a way that is constructive and professional.

This book is about sharing ideas. I've attempted to describe my personal transition as a math teacher: that I now believe students learn by constructing their own knowledge; that I believe my role as a teacher is to provide rich, engaging mathematical situations for students and to provide a safe atmosphere in which they can explore mathematics; that I want my students to feel free to make conjectures and test them out with data that they gather; that I want my students to be able to communicate about mathematics and to work together with other students, *all* other students; that I believe students often learn better in small groups than they do individually or in a large group; that I believe there are many different ways to assess student progress and many of them are more valid than traditional tests; that I believe developing number sense is much more important than developing the ability to compute with pencil and paper; that I believe writing helps students learn mathematics and helps teachers assess student learning.

I've also shared a few of the things I've tried over the years that have made this transition happen. I've been a middle school math teacher for over twenty-three years. During the last few years, I've incorporated more new ideas into my teaching than in the previous twenty years combined. I have never worked harder both in and out of the classroom, *but I've never enjoyed teaching more, nor have I ever felt better about what my students are learning.* I will continue to make transitions in my teaching, and I'm confident that my students and I will continue to learn together. I wish you the same joy and sense of accomplishment in your teaching.

References

Lindquist, Mary, ed. 1989. *Results from the Fourth Mathematics Assessment of the National Assessment of Educational Progress.* Reston, VA: National Council of Teachers of Mathematics.

Mathematics Framework for California Public Schools. 1992. Sacramento, CA: California State Department of Education.

National Council of Teachers of Mathematics. 1989. *Curriculum and Evaluation Standards for School Mathematics.* Reston, VA: National Council of Teachers of Mathematics.

National Research Council. 1989. *Everybody Counts: A Report to the Nation on the Future of Mathematics Education.* Washington DC: National Academy Press.

———. 1990. *Reshaping School Mathematics: A Philosophy and Framework for Curriculum.* Washington DC: National Academy Press.

Paulos, John. 1988. *Innumeracy: Mathematical Illiteracy and Its Consequences.* New York: Hill and Wang.

Resnick, Lauren. 1987. *Education and Learning to Think.* Washington DC: National Academy Press.

United States Department of Education. National Commission on Excellence in Education. 1983. *A Nation at Risk: The Imperative for Educational Reform.* Washington DC: GPO.